The Telegraph Style Guide

Why have a house style?

It is important to provide conformity not just in newspapers but on websites, and to ensure that we are all speaking and writing the same language.

To echo the introduction to a previous *Telegraph* style guide:

"Its aims are accuracy, immediacy, clarity and readability. And the greatest of these is not clarity but accuracy."

The **Telegraph**
Style Guide

The official guide to house style for *The Daily Telegraph*, its supplements and magazines; *The Sunday Telegraph*, its supplements and magazines; and Telegraph.co.uk

edited by Simon Heffer

researched by Philip Reynolds

cartoons by MATT

First published in Great Britain
2010 by Aurum Press Ltd
7 Greenland Street, London NW1 0ND
www.aurumpress.co.uk

Every effort has been made to trace the copyright holders of material
quoted in this book. If application is made in writing to the publisher,
any omissions will be included in future editions.

A catalogue record for this book is available from the British Library.

ISBN: 978 1 84513 571 3

3 5 7 9 10 8 6 4
2010 2012 2014 2013 2011

Designed and typeset in Mrs Eaves by M Rules
Printed in Great Britain by Clays Ltd, St Ives plc

CONTENTS

FOREWORD *by Simon Heffer*

The Daily Telegraph has had a style book, in some incarnation or another, for decades. When I first joined the paper just before it left Fleet Street in the mid-1980s there were battered copies of an ancient edition floating around, and it was not, I think, reprinted until the late 1990s. A newspaper style book is not something so straightforward as a dictionary of usage, though it is that, too. It has to accommodate fads, fashions and the peculiar proper names of people and places in the news. Therefore, by the end of the first decade of the 21st century much that was important and relevant 10 years earlier had changed or had been superseded. I rewrote the style book in 2008 and my colleague Philip Reynolds, *The Daily Telegraph*'s meticulous chief reader, has incorporated my own updates since then into this new, expanded and revised edition.

Unlike previous versions, this is available to the general public. We at the *Telegraph* know how strongly our readers feel about language, and how cross they get when we abuse it. We are a quality newspaper and, as such, we seek to appeal to quality customers. Such people know when we get it wrong. The publication of our style book shows that we are serious about the task of improving quality, and prepared to be held to account for our mistakes. Producing a newspaper every day is an enormous job, and it would be a sign that it was produced by robots if no mistake ever got through: but we try to keep them to a minimum.

We also hope that the book will be useful to people other than for spotting where we journalists have broken our own rules. It should help clarify many points that arise in all our minds when we write letters or emails, and when we wish to be correct in all respects. It may even settle arguments at home and in the pub. Last but not least, we have tried to make it interesting, informative and entertaining. We hope we have succeeded, and that, having read it, you will not only have refreshed your memory about the niceties of our mother tongue but will also have passed a few hours enjoyably and profitably.

Simon Heffer
Associate Editor, *The Daily Telegraph*
20 September 2010

INTRODUCTION by Philip Reynolds

In his book *The House the Berrys Built: Inside the Telegraph*, Duff Hart-Davis recounts a story from the late Fifties concerning Elizabeth Taylor. On arrival at Heathrow airport and in response to questions from reporters asking how she was, Miss Taylor replied: "I'm feeling like a million dollars."

The next morning *The Daily Telegraph* dutifully reported Miss Taylor's comment but saw fit to include alongside the quote a currency conversion into sterling, as laid down by the style guide of the day. "I'm feeling like a million dollars (£357,000)."

Such strict adherence to the rules was, in this instance, ridiculous, if not a little amusing, depicting Miss Taylor in not quite as good fettle as she thought. But it does serve to show the importance of style in the *Telegraph* firmament.

A newspaper develops a "house style" that is recognisable and, hopefully, in tune with its readership. Such style is what makes *The Daily Telegraph* and its sister *The Sunday Telegraph*, and the website Telegraph.co.uk distinctive and popular.

It is axiomatic that grammar, punctuation and spelling must be correct. Words are the tools of a journalist and their proper use is the best way to convey a message lucidly and effectively, lest gallimaufry result.

The *Oxford English Dictionary* includes in its description of the noun *style*: a particular procedure by which something is done; a way of using language; and a distinctive appearance. Arguably, all of these are apposite in the corporate enterprise of producing a newspaper seven days a week and maintaining a website for 24 hours of each of these days.

The Telegraph Media Group produces newspapers and a website that are rightly thought to be part of the "quality" media. As such they ought to be written in a way that distinguishes them from their rivals, in particular the "red tops" or tabloids, free from hackneyed phrases and sensationalism.

However, things can be taken too far, as the splash headline on Friday, 8 February, 1952 shows, when the Queen returned to London to assume monarchal duties following the death of George VI, her father. "The Queen in London: Phones her Mother" said the headline in 90pt.

But does this mean the *Telegraph*'s standards shift with time? No. However, things change and the *Telegraph* has always been happy to reflect these changes, providing they reflect the tenor and quality of *The Daily Telegraph* and its associated publications and media.

Language, especially the English language, does not stand still. Uses and meanings change over generations. This is not to say that the *Telegraph* bends in the breeze of linguistic vagaries, but it does acknowledge progress and its resultant impact on life.

What might have been frowned upon when the updated style book was presented to journalists at 135 Fleet Street in January 1971 would seem outmoded to today's generation of *Telegraph* journalists nearly 40 years on.

A perusal of that edition shows that "billion" and "disc jockey" were among the banned words and phrases. But in 2010, a billion is no longer a mind-boggling amount to today's readers and is the only accurate way of describing a country's deficit or an individual's wealth.

And in the second decade of the 21st century, for many, the people playing the discs are as much a star as the artists whose discs they are playing.

Then there is the digital revolution, which has transformed the media over the last 20 years. Websites are integral to media groups' operations, visited by tens of thousands of people every day. But what makes a good headline in the newspaper does not necessarily apply on the web, due to the exigencies of search engine criteria. The algorithms of Google will not be as appreciative of a sub-editor's gentle pun as many of the *Telegraph*'s readers.

In the world of SEO (Search Engine Optimisation), the web likes things to be as literal as possible. In many ways, this has seen things turn full circle since Col Arthur B Sleigh published the first edition of the paper on June 29 1855. "Despatches from the seat of war", ran the only headline on the front page. Perhaps today such a story on the internet would read: "Crimea: reports from the front line".

Certain things, however, are immutable, and one of these is the glorious tradition of *The Daily Telegraph*, the aims of which are beautifully encapsulated by the late Lord Burnham, a former proprietor of the paper, in his book *Peterborough Court*. "So much is done today to obviate the necessity of thinking of any kind, to titillate the palate of the newspaper reader with highly spiced material, that it must be comforting to think that so many people of both sexes and all ages will every day buy a newspaper which, whatever its faults of omission and commission, and there are many, can only appeal to those who are reasonably serious-minded and who take a responsible view of the importance of being well informed on things that really matter."

It is hoped this style guide will contribute to the continuing aims of this noble sentiment.

By the way, Miss Taylor would no doubt have been pleased to learn that, due to the pound's fall against the dollar, at one point her feelings had appreciated in value to as much as £643,000.

BASIC PRINCIPLES

That's tautology, you foolish ass!

THE WRITER'S RESPONSIBILITY

It cannot be emphasised strongly enough that conformity with style, accurate use of the English language and accuracy in use of facts, quotes and other information are the responsibility of the writer.

No writer should expect his or her editors to spot mistakes or solecisms or to be there to correct them. The responsibility for any errors that end up being published will lie solely with the author. It is highly unprofessional for any writer to leave any aspect of his or her work to be clarified by any other journalist.

For this reason especially, as well as in respect for the integrity of the writer whose byline will appear on the published piece of writing, no changes of fact should be made to copy after it has been filed without the knowledge of the writer. Nomenclature, etc should be changed only when what has been written is in obvious breach of house style.

There is no better maxim than the one taught to journalists when they are setting out: "Who, what, where, when, how" should form the cornerstones of every story. The "Why" may well provide the thrust of the story but the first five criteria must never be neglected.

Convey the message as you would speak it. Few people who are worth listening to speak in sentences of more than 30 words. Try to avoid multiple subordinate clauses as they breed confusion. Concision is one of the greatest virtues of expression and, therefore, of good writing.

Never take for granted the reader's understanding of a subject. It is not insulting to set things out simply and logically. Do not, however, patronise by remarks such as "the author Charles Dickens": with an educated readership there are certain assumptions about their general knowledge that we can make. Remember, though, that with an educated readership mistakes are easily spotted, and the publication and author are easily diminished by them.

Every article should be self-contained, with an explanation, however brief, of what has gone before. Always presume that an intelligent, widely read reader has recently been on a desert island, without benefit of media.

Aim for common sense and question apparent nonsenses, such as pike in village ponds that swallow small dogs. Use your own yardstick as to what is feasible but do check. Good journalism at all levels is largely about the development of judgment.

Be temperate in language, especially in journalistic headlines. Keeping a sense of proportion — recognising that "storms" and "fury" are often merely disagreements or differences of opinion — shows balance and maturity.

Profanities are always to be avoided in news reporting and to be used only when absolutely essential in other coverage. The most obscene swear words are never to be used in any circumstances. Language of a sexually explicit nature should only be used when essential — such as in certain court reports or features about health or relationships — and never gratuitously or for effect.

The word partner, when used to denote an unmarried cohabitee, is to be avoided unless all other descriptions are inappropriate. Use girlfriend, boyfriend, companion, lover, mistress, concubine, friend or any other apposite word. **See also banned words and phrases in the glossary.**

It is essential that journalists writing news stories recall the distinction between news and comment. One can be free with opinion (within the law) in comment articles: but there is no place for it in news stories. On news pages readers expect to see facts, unvarnished by observations.

Avoid tabloid constructions and agency-speak. "Television addict, Mansfield butcher John Smith" should be John Smith, a butcher from Mansfield who is addicted to television. Also, NOT: London's West End; the famous anything (if it is famous there is no need to say so). Steer clear of words such as "spotted" and "dubbed", and use "saw" and "called" or "nicknamed". **Further examples of such horrors are to be found in the glossary.**

Be wary of the ways in which agencies seek to "classify" people. One is to identify a person as a grandparent. They may be grandparents in their early forties and a false picture can be drawn. Unless it's relevant, stick to the age. Unless you are certain something is exclusive to your story, avoid the construction "told *The Daily Telegraph*". Even then use extremely sparingly: it is a vulgar tabloid device and much more easily replaced by the word "said". Suspicion is advisable, too, in giving the value of houses. It is, these days, at best theoretical.

Attribute everything. Without care, it is easy when putting a subject's words into reported speech to render his or her claims and opinions into statements of fact. Even if sources are anonymous, it is important to source in its opening paragraph any claim on which a story is constructed: **otherwise, why should the reader read on?**

Agency copy - needs to be (re)written in *Telegraph* style.

Avoid clichés. They cripple news stories with their tiredness and the laziness with which they are used. Fashionable phrases rarely have a usefulness that lasts more than a few weeks.

They are also often glib and inaccurate and are never an acceptable substitute for proper descriptions of events. A cliché or pun in a headline may be new to you, but it quite possibly isn't to the readers: avoid tired old jokes of the "Life's a beach" variety.

Please bear in mind that newspapers publish and printers print. *The Daily Telegraph* and its associated media do not print stories: they publish them.

Adherence to these and all the other rules set out in this guide will not in itself create a first-class journalist or indeed a first-class newspaper or first-class website, but it will be the start of such process.

GRAMMAR AND SYNTAX

'I'm not an escapee, I'm an escaper'

TENSES

Whenever we are reporting something that has already happened yesterday or before we use the past tense. This includes official reports, surveys and studies.

Having so started we must adhere to that style. "The report said that if nothing were done, things would get worse", not "The report said that if nothing is done, things will get worse". Similarly, in reported speech we should use "had" instead of "has", as in "but nothing had been done".

If the report is published today (i.e. the day of publication) we should say "the report says that if nothing is done, things will get worse", etc. Switching tenses in a story is confusing and sloppy.

May and might: "may" is the present and future tense, "might" is the imperfect, perfect and pluperfect, so use in reported speech. I may go: he said he might go. "He may have been on the plane that crashed" means he could be missing. "He might have been on the plane that crashed" means that chance intervened and he wasn't.

Moods: contrary to popular belief, the subjunctive has not died completely, and some surviving usages would adorn not only feature writing but also some news reports. The mood was historically used with verbs of volition and command ("he ordered that he be brought in" and "she wishes that she were at home") and with conditional clauses ("he agreed provided that he be not quoted"), and it is not incorrect to use them today.

Americans make a fetish of them. Note that the imperfect of the subjunctive "were" is "was", so you would write "she wished she was at home". Usages like "I order that he come" are perhaps a little rarefied for modern times: use this mood only when it seems natural.

Hyphens. These are frequently misused. See glossary for a guide but a rough and ready test is to speak the words. Where hyphens are used there is a quickening of pace. As an example: "He was a member of the middle class. But he belongs to a middle-class club." See glossary for an exposition of this subject.

Dashes should not be used as routine replacement for commas, but they are useful to indicate the written equivalent of a change of tone in speech (the attack was unexpected – it came at noon instead of dawn – and the enemy outnumbered them).

Dashes also help to avoid confusion by enclosing a series of words punctuated by commas. "Reporters face many problems — censorship, the pressure of time, shortage of space — when they work overseas."

That: make special note of the importance of the word "that", which the tabloids have all but removed from the English language in its role as a conjunction, as in: "he claimed the prize but he claimed that he was the winner."

This applies to all those words like "propose", "recommend", "suggest", etc. Taking the "that" out makes the reader stumble over the sense. It is not needed after the verb "said". (See also "that" in the glossary.) "That" as a relative pronoun, and its correct usage in relation to "which" is dealt with in the glossary too.

Adjectives: adjectives other than the purely and basically descriptive have little place in news stories, and little more (other than occasionally for comic or ironic effect) in feature writing. Highly adjectival writing is a mainstay of tabloid journalism.

Collective nouns: these are usually singular, but there are good reasons not to impose a rigid rule. Sport provides many examples (England were all out for 50). Let common sense rule (the Government was in trouble; the Cabinet took their places in a sombre mood). Aim for consistency in similar references throughout a story, but this does not mean that different collective nouns cannot be treated in different ways within a story.

THE TELEGRAPH STYLE GUIDE

Commas impede the flow of a sentence, but omitting them may change its meaning. Omitting the commas in "The minister's wife Mary was there" suggests polygamy. If he has only one wife, make it "The minister's wife, Mary, was there".

Commas are needed before "and", "but" and "for" in compound sentences, unless the clauses they precede are very short (John was hungry, but his hostess insisted on reading a book before cooking lunch. He ate but his wife fasted). Commas are used between pairs or series of adjectives, but should be dropped if the words cannot properly be joined by "and" (a cold, grey dawn greeted the awakening old prisoner).

Hanging participles Beware the curse of the hanging participle. It is perfectly acceptable to employ a participle at the beginning of a sentence, but used incorrectly it can cause confusion and unintended amusement. The rule is to keep the adjectival clause – the descriptive part – adjacent to what it refers to: the subject of the sentence. For example, 'Singing in the bath, the stress of life seemed a million miles away to John' is inelegant. Though we probably know what is meant, strictly speaking it is the stress that is singing here. 'Singing in the bath, John felt the stress of life to be a million miles away' is better.

BANNED WORDS AND PHRASES

'My crime was to use the word "gaol" in the *Telegraph*'

This is a list that is liable to grow.

ace is acceptable when describing a card, it is not to be used to describe someone who excels at something.

across: the slang usage of someone "being across" something to suggest he is cognisant of it is banned.

ahead of (before is shorter).

as of now

as to

autopsy (Americanism).

bid (when we mean attempt).

blasted

bloodbath

boardroom antics

boffin

breathtaking

bubbly (both for champagne and young women).

budget airline

chairperson, chair (chairman is correct English).

choke back tears

clampdown

closet (as an adjective).

coffers

come out (for homosexual people).

crackdown

crashed out

crowd pleaser

dad

deep throat

disgraced managers, innocent victims and all their tribe are
out.

doctors fought to save

dog-whistle politics

doom and gloom

entitled (when we are referring to something's name).

epitome of

Europhobe

fall pregnant

fat cat

fighting for his life

frail grannies

fuelled (for anything that does not involve fuel).

going forward

green light

gunned down

heartbreak

hit series

hinge

hike (when we mean a rise).

huge

iconic

jaw-dropping

kid (for child).

launched (for anything that is not a boat, spacecraft or projectile. Book launch is acceptable as a noun).

loaned (no such verb: use lent).

local residents are residents.

luxury (as an adjective: very tabloid).

mass exodus

meet with

mission creep

mum

mum-to-be

mystery callers

nation's favourite

order of magnitude

over, when the sense is more than.

overly

perfect storm

perverted Scout leaders

posh

prior to

probe (when we mean inquiry).

quizzed is not an acceptable substitute for questioned.

revellers

rubber-chicken circuit

rubbish (as a verb).

scam

set to, as in "The Church of England was last night set to ..." or "The FA is set to name", is to be avoided at all costs in text and headlines.

shocked

simply (as in "simply fill in the form").

slammed is acceptable for a door, but not as a metaphor for criticism.

slashed (instead of cut).

snapped (of a photograph).

soar (unless it physically is rising steeply upwards).

sparked (when we mean caused or provoked).

stressed (when we mean emphasised).

stretcher – it is not a verb.

stunned (unless the subject really is unconscious).

stunning

tad

toff

toilet

trademark (except when referring to trademarks); never refer to someone "wearing his trademark hat", etc.

try and (it is try to).

U-turns are reversals, about-turns or rethinks.

Avoid clichés, especially horrors like "a furious row erupted" and "massive heart attack". "Brutal murder/rape" is a tautology: we should assume all such crimes are brutal.

Watch out for hackneyed expressions such as ordeal, feisty, legendary, lifestyle, major, massive, mammoth, bumper, bonanza, boost, effectively, pinta, copycat, lookalike, tit-for-tat and substitute proper words, where the word or phrase is not redundant.

Phrases taken from film titles, such as home alone, are overused. Instead of saying that children are left "home alone" say "left alone". Our readers know that parents whose children have been murdered or otherwise killed are "devastated" and "heartbroken" and we should not stupidly say that they are.

Picking Blackberries

NAMES AND TITLES

'Very nice to see you, Mr Loaf'

GENERALLY

At first mention use the person's name in full. Then use Mr, Mrs, Miss. Ms is permissible out of courtesy when it is the title that the person herself requests.

Once someone is dead and the funeral has taken place he or she is referred to by forename and surname at the first mention, or a title if he or she had one, then just by his or her surname in subsequent mentions. Show sensitivity in references to murder victims, leaving them with their honorifics during an investigation and any subsequent court case. The following rules apply strictly to the news and comment sections of the paper. As discussed above, sports will not use honorifics for players but will for officials.

The features pages will have their own more informal style, though the discretion and judgment of executives are important in defining the boundaries of rectitude in this context. Common sense is the best guide.

Children under the age of 18 are referred to by their forenames and surnames at first mention and by their forenames later.

Minors convicted of a crime are, in cases where the courts permit them to be named, referred to only by their surname.

Married women who do not use their husbands' names take Miss in later mentions. If necessary, indicate marital status as in: "Mary Smith, the actress, and her son were injured. Miss Smith, who is married to Dr John Doe, said ..."

Defendants in criminal court cases, other than those already serving prison sentences or who have entered a plea of guilty, are to be referred to with their honorific Mr, Mrs or Miss: the newspapers and website should share the court's presumption of innocence.

On conviction they lose the honorific, although if cleared on appeal they reclaim it. If more than one person with the same surname is in court, use forenames to distinguish them.

Sportsmen and women, actors and entertainers do not take the honorific when being written about in their professional context on the Sports, Arts or Features pages.

However, when written about in the news pages, except in the context of an on-field incident during a sporting fixture or in a story related to their professional activities, they should be afforded the same courtesy as all others.

We extend the Mr/Mrs rule to **all foreigners**: Mr Sarkozy, Mrs Merkel, Miss Dati.

Knights and peers keep their titles at first mention and thereafter.

Doctors, academics, Servicemen and women, police and fire officers and the clergy keep their titles at first mention after which the normal rules apply.

Doctors remain Dr and **professors** Prof.

Private soldiers remain Ptes unless their regimental custom decrees that they shall be called Guardsman, Fusilier or Rifleman, etc.

A Major General or Lt General should not be abbreviated to Gen, which is the correct abbreviation only for a four-star general; they should be Maj Gen and Lt Gen respectively. Similarly, differentiate Lieutenant Colonel (Lt Col) from Colonel (Col). There is no rank of Brigadier General in the British Army but it still exists in certain others, and should be abbreviated Brig Gen. The rank of Major is never abbreviated. (See Army.)

Senior police officers (of Insp rank and above) become Mr at second mention. The abbreviations Pc and Sgt are used for lower ranks at all mentions. Other abbreviations are: Det Con, Det Sgt, Insp, Det Insp, Chief Insp, Det Chief Insp, Supt, Det Supt, Chief Supt, Det Chief Supt, Dept Asst Commissioner, Asst Chief Constable, Dept Chief Constable. Commander, Commissioner and Chief Constable out in full.

ECCLESIASTICAL TITLES

By convention, the names of bishops and archbishops always follow the title of their office: the Archbishop of Canterbury, Dr Rowan Williams (use Christian and surname). Then Dr Williams or the Archbishop.

Not all high ecclesiastics have doctorates, but Dr should be used when it is correct. Accepted Anglican usages include: the Bishop of Someshire, the Rt Rev John Smith (later the bishop or Bishop Smith).

The Bishop-Suffragan of Sometown, the Rt Rev John Smith (later the bishop or Bishop Smith).

The Very Rev John Smith, Dean of Sometown (later the dean or Dr or Mr Smith); the Ven John Smith, Archdeacon of Sometown (Dr or Mr); the Rev John Smith, vicar of St Mary's, Sometown (Mr Smith); the Rev John Smith, rector of Someville (Mr Smith).

Never refer to the Rev Smith, or Rev John Smith without the definite article. At first mention always use his first name or, at least, the initials.

Canons, prebendaries, deans and archdeacons are sometimes given emeritus rank on retirement and retain their titles.

Otherwise they revert to "the Rev". The terms "rector" and "vicar" are not interchangeable but have different significance according to the parish concerned. In the Anglican Church, only certain high Anglicans choose to be known as "Father" or to be referred to as a "priest".

Roman Catholic styles are flexible except that Dr is never used for bishops and archbishops. Mgr (for monsignor) is correct. Cardinal-Archbishop is seldom used in Britain.

These styles are accepted: Cardinal Smith, Archbishop of Westminster. The Archbishop of Westminster, Cardinal Smith.

The Roman Catholic Bishop of Sometown, the Rt Rev John Smith (later the bishop or Bishop Smith). We should not automatically refer later to bishops as Mgr Smith. Being a monsignor does not imply one is a bishop, nor being a bishop imply that one is a monsignor.

Monsignor refers to an honorific status granted by the Pope: i.e. Mgr John Smith, Roman Catholic parish priest of St Peter's, Sometown (later Mgr Smith). Do not use 'Roman Catholic Cardinal Smith' (the use of 'cardinal' establishes that he is Roman Catholic). Formally, bishops are the Rt Rev and archbishops the Most Rev and these styles may be used. In Ireland all bishops are the Most Rev.

The Rev John Smith, Roman Catholic parish priest of St Peter's, Sometown, or Father John Smith, Roman Catholic parish priest (later Father or Fr Smith).

The Pope. Pope John XXIII or Pope Pius IX for earlier popes.

Moderator: he is the Moderator of the General Assembly of the Church of Scotland, not Moderator of the Church of Scotland.

ROYALTY

British Royalty: the Queen is always just that. Queen Elizabeth the Queen Mother ceased to be "Queen Mother" on her death and it is as incorrect now to refer to her as such as it would be still to call her deceased husband "the King".

Like Queens Alexandra and Mary before her (who were both Queens Mother after the deaths of their husbands) she should now be referred to as Queen Elizabeth.

To avoid the possibility of confusion with the Sovereign or even with Queen Elizabeth I, she should be referred to at first mention as "the late Queen Elizabeth the Queen Mother" and subsequently as "Queen Elizabeth".

In news stories, other members of the Royal family should be referred to by their full title at first mention and then by their short title. Princes or Princesses who have had a higher honour bestowed on them by the Sovereign should be referred to by that title.

For example, Prince Philip is the Duke of Edinburgh on first mention and then the Duke. Prince Charles should be referred to as the Prince of Wales at first mention and then as the Prince. Princess Anne should be the Princess Royal at first mention and then the Princess. Diana, Princess of Wales, is never "Princess Diana".

The term "a Royal" and "the Royals" is tabloid and is to be avoided. Use instead "a member of the Royal family" and "the Royal family".

In headlines use "Prince" instead of "William" or "Harry".

Foreign royalty: at first mention the King of Spain or the Queen of Denmark, or Prince Ernst of Hanover or Princess Charlotte of Mecklenburg, or the Grand Duke of Luxembourg, subsequently the King, Queen, Prince, Princess and Grand Duke, with initial caps.

NOBILITY, BARONETS, KNIGHTAGE

Titles of nobility are, in descending order: duke, marquess (not marquis except for foreign titles and a few ancient Scottish titles), earl, viscount and baron. Give the formal title except for barons at first mention (Marquess of Bath, the Earl of Snowdon) but then use Lord Bath, Lord Snowdon.

Dukes are always dukes and do not become Lord xxxx.

Barons, except in the announcement of new baronies, are always Lord xxxx.

Baronesses however are described by their full title at first mention and are Lady xxxx subsequently. This distinguishes life peeresses from the handful of hereditary baronies that descend through the female as well as through the male line, and whose holders (when female) are always described as "Lady Smith".

Some peers have a territorial designation as part of their name. When it is not part of their name the territorial designation should not be given except when a new title is being reported.

Peers are obliged to include a territorial designation in their title when there is another peerage with an identical name. Thus when Chris Patten was ennobled he had to become Lord Patten of Barnes, as his contemporary John Patten had already become Lord Patten.

It is important to give the full title in reports to avoid confusion. Lord Patten has the territorial designation "of Wincanton" but it is not part of his title, and nor, as the first Patten peerage to be created, is he obliged to use it. Lord Patten of Barnes, as the second creation with that name, is.

Who's Who helpfully includes territorial designations in CAPITALS when they form part of the name of the peer: e.g., LORD PATTEN OF BARNES.

For second mention he may be called Lord Patten, unless there is a danger of confusing him with his namesake.

The wife of a marquess is a marchioness, of an earl a countess, of a viscount a viscountess. Use Lady at second and subsequent mentions. But the wife of a baron is always Lady at first and subsequent mentions.

Some women other than life peeresses hold hereditary or life peerages in their own right. Their husbands do not take their rank or therefore, a title (the Countess of Someshire and her husband John Smith).

Eldest sons of dukes, marquesses and earls take by courtesy the father's second title, assuming there is one. The Duke of Bedford's son is the Marquess of Tavistock. Lord Tavistock's elder son, if he has one, can use the third title of the Duke, and he therefore is Lord Howland.

Younger sons of dukes and marquesses use their forenames after the courtesy title "Lord" and before the family surname, which is not usually the same as the peerage title itself (a younger son of the Duke of Bedford, for example, might be Lord John Russell).

These people are not peers — a designation that suggests they hold a peerage itself — even in headlines.

At subsequent references he is "Lord John", never "Lord Russell".

The use of Hon before the names of other children of peers (the Hon John Smith) is now normally restricted to formal social circumstances. Avoid in all copy.

The designation "Lady" is used with a forename by the daughters of dukes, marquesses and earls, before the family surname.

The style is Lady Mary Russell and then Lady Mary, never, in such cases, Lady Russell.

The wives of younger sons of dukes and marquesses use "Lady" with their husbands' forenames, as in Lady John Russell. At second mention, she is Lady John, never Lady Russell.

Wives of baronets and knights are styled, for example, Lady Smith (Sir William and Lady Smith).

When the name is a common one and no other form of identification is convenient, the form Lady (William) Smith is available, but the brackets must be used.

Knights' widows may be identified as Lady (Mary) Smith.

The widow of a baronet whose son, the present baronet, is married is Mary, Lady Smith.

Should the wife of a baronet or knight be the daughter of a duke, marquess or earl then she will still use her rank and be Lady Mary Smith rather than Lady Smith.

The term dowager is correct for the earliest surviving widow of a peer, but it is widely disliked because of pejorative connotations. The form Mary, Viscountess Someshire (later Lady Someshire) is generally used for widowed or divorced women.

The daughters of dukes, marquesses and earls retain the title "Lady" on marriage to a commoner — Lady Mary Someshire becomes Lady Mary Smith, wife of John Smith.

Never refer to Lady Mary Someshire unless she is the daughter of a duke, marquess or earl.

Foreign barons, counts and marquises do not become Lord xxxx.

MINOR OFFICES AND ADMINISTRATIVE AND COMMERCIAL APPOINTMENTS

Job descriptions such as managing director, chairman and chief executive all take lower case.

Also: John Smith, the Sometown coroner. John Smith, the magistrate. Sir John Smith, chairman of Amalgamated Industries. John Smith, general secretary of the TUC.

In local government, John Smith, the Mayor of Sometown, or John Smith, Mayor of Sometown. But lower-case leaders of councils and chairmen of general committees.

FOREIGN NOMENCLATURE

Imam: leader of prayers in a mosque, also the title of various Muslim leaders. Islam does not have a priesthood, so refer to clerics not priests. "Clergy" is acceptable.

Arab names: widely differing customs and pronunciations in Arabic-speaking countries make it impossible to lay down rigid rules for transliteration into English.

Follow established style or usage when it exists (Gaddafi) or any known preference of the person concerned. When in doubt, repeat the whole name rather than guess at the proper form for use at second mention.

The definite article al (which can appear as el, ul, an, ud or in many other forms) should be dropped at second mention or when used with a title but only when it stands alone or is hyphenated.

The word for son (ibn or bin) should be dropped at second reference (Abdul bin Rashid becomes Mr Rashid), but the word abu (father of) should be retained (Abdul Moheen Abu Maizer becomes Mr Abu Maizer).

In some cases, the second name serves to identify merely the family or clan to which a person belongs. The first name identifies that person more precisely. It is for this reason that Saddam Hussein is referred to as Saddam, not Hussein, and when alive was not Mr Hussein.

Titles of rulers – King, Prince, Sheikh, Sultan – should be followed only by the personal name (often the first in a long sequence) and the name of the country. The title Emir is sometimes translated as Prince, but usage varies from one country to another.

Haji is a title used by men who have made the pilgrimage to Mecca. It should not be preceded by Mr.

If the outcome of an election is disputed be cautious about bestowing titles including prime minister and president. If in doubt use 'Mr' or 'Mrs' instead.

Asian names: the rule for Chinese and Korean names is that the surname comes first and the given name second, but some anglicised Chinese use their surname last, sometimes with initials only, as in the shipowner CH Tung.

Chinese mainland given names are one word only, as in (Deng) Xiaoping. Hong Kong Chinese and Korean given names are hyphenated, as in (Roh) Tae-woo.

South-east Asian Chinese given names are two words as in (Lee) Kuan Yew. Taiwanese are usually hyphenated.

In Thai and Malay, the given name comes first followed by a surname or patronymic, but the given name is used after first mention as in Mahathir Mohamad (his father was Mohamad something). Cambodians, Vietnamese, Laotians and Burmese also use this system, but sometimes in reverse order. (Aung San Suu Kyi's father was Aung San. She is Miss Suu Kyi on second mention.)

Indonesians, more often than not, have only one name, as in Suharto.

Indian, Pakistani and Bangladeshi names are usually in the normal order (given name, then surname), but many South Indians use an initial only instead of a first name (this is because the first name is a patronymic, often about 30 letters long). A few Indians (usually tribal people) have only one name.

Foreign appointments: President Smith, subsequently the president or Mr Smith.

As there are currently two Presidents Bush living, distinguish between George W and George HW.

Senior office holders should have their offices capped up where they are not translations from another language: thus Hillary Clinton, the Secretary of State, but Bernard Kouchner, the French foreign minister.

Use initial capitals for titles and institutions but not bodies that are sub-sets of institutions: thus Senator Smith, chairman of the Senate foreign relations committee. Representative John Smith of Maine. Senator John Smith (Republican, Maine) only in stories with many American political references. Never Congressman John Smith as this could refer to either house of Congress. Senators should be accorded their title at first mention, to become "Mr", "Mrs" or "Miss" subsequently.

Chancellor Angela Merkel of Germany, subsequently the chancellor or Mrs Merkel.

Premier is used after names only for heads of government of Australian states and Canadian provinces (John Smith, Premier of Queensland) and Communist countries in which job descriptions extend to titles such as "first deputy premier".

We have adopted the Pinyin system of romanising Chinese words, characterised by its use of x, zh, q, etc at the beginning of syllables.

Taiwan names and place-names continue to take the system used by the Nationalist government: we do not turn Chiang Kai-shek into Jiang Jieshi, etc.

This means that the following spellings are correct:

Places:
Beijing (not Peking).
Nanjing (not Nanking).
Chongqing (not Chungking).
Guangzhou (not Canton).
Hangzhou (not Hangchow).
Tianjin (not Tientsin).

People: Mao Tse-tung bucks the Pinyin trend and keeps his old name-form, rather than Mao Zedong;

Otherwise: Liu Shaoqi (no longer Liu Shao-chi); Lin Biao (not Lin Piao); Zhou Enlai (not Chou En-Lai); Jiang Qing (not Chiang Ching).
Nationalist Chinese names:
Sun Yat-sen (not Sun Zhongshan);
Chiang Kai-shek (not Jiang Jieshi or Jiang Kai-shek);
President Lee Teng-hui.

Names of regions:
Hong Kong (not Xianggang);
Tibet (not Xinzhang);
Lhasa (not Lasa);

Taiwan:
Taipei (not Taibei);
Kaohsiung (not Gaoxiong);
Macao (not Macau).

COURTS AND CRIME

This section is not a legal textbook. If you have doubts on legal points refer to the in-house lawyer, the news desk or your line manager.

Accuracy is not always enough. In certain circumstances it may be held that the publication of factually correct material is malicious, irresponsible or timed to facilitate ill-feeling.

Accused: may be used for stylistic purposes in a long report but the first and normal usage is "the defendant". Use names when possible unless this would lead to identification, by "jigsaw" (piecing facts together) or other means, of a victim of a sex offence.

As mentioned earlier, the *Telegraph* shares the presumption of innocence of a defendant: so Mr, Mrs or Miss Smith, unless he or she is a convicted criminal still serving a sentence or has pleaded guilty.

Allegations: at trials should always be attributed to a named or otherwise identified person.

Anonymity: it is normally a contempt to publish anything that would identify the alleged victim of rape, attempted rape, aiding, abetting, counselling or procuring rape or attempted rape, and incitement to rape. The anonymity rules were extended in 1992 to cover other alleged sex offences: check with the lawyer.

The restrictions may be lifted by courts or if the written consent of the victim has been obtained without duress. The restrictions apply from the moment the accusation is made, even if the attacker is unknown and at large. They apply for the lifetime of the victim.

Contempt of court: crime stories need not be completely emasculated even after an arrest, but care is needed. Do not report anything that may be the subject of dispute at a trial. Do not identify those arrested with any gang whose activities have been described earlier in a story.

When approaching crime stories, do not presume that the police always arrest the right people. Leave a gap in the narrative between the account of, say, the raid on the bank and the gunmen's escape to a waiting car and the account of a car (not the car) being halted and four men, still presumed to be innocent, being detained.

Descriptions of alleged criminals may have to be deleted from stories after an arrest; a juror who remembers a graphic description of the 6ft 4in man with a red beard who ran away after shooting a policeman is unlikely to have an open mind about the 6ft 4in man in the dock.

Warnings about fugitives being **armed and dangerous** should always be attributed to a named senior police officer.

Also beware of referring to a defendant's previous convictions during a trial or hearing. Do not, unless directed to by a judge or magistrate.

Headlines such as "Murder remand" are dangerous. The defence may admit that someone was killed but deny that it was murder.

Coroners' courts: the coroner's task is to ascertain the cause of a death by holding an inquest in open court unless he or she thinks it in the national interest to hold it in camera. He may sit alone or may summon a jury. Coroners need not be lawyers. They may be doctors. They operate an inquisitorial rather than an adversarial system. The coroner records a verdict; a coroner's jury returns a verdict. The laws of contempt apply.

COURTS AND JUDICIARY

Court of Appeal: its judges include the Master of the Rolls and the Lords Justices of Appeal who are not Law Lords. Refer to the Master of the Rolls, Sir John Smith, and to Lord Justice Smith.

County courts: Judge John Smith QC said at Sometown county court. Later references to Judge Smith or the judge.

Crown Court: the Crown Court, of which the Old Bailey is a part, sits in towns and cities throughout England and Wales. Refer to Sometown Crown Court.

There are three ranks of judge who sit in Crown Courts:

High Court judges: Mr Justice Smith (never Judge Smith). Off-duty they are referred to by the title they receive on appointment, as Sir John Smith, the High Court judge.

Circuit judges: Judge Smith. If there are two Judge Smiths then they will be known by their forenames as well, to avoid confusion: Judge John Smith, Judge James Smith.

Recorders: practising lawyers who sit as part-time judges. The recorder, John Smith QC, said at Sometown Crown Court. Later references to the recorder.

All kinds of Crown Court judges may be referred to as judges in heads and intros.

Apart from High Court judges, they should be given their titles and designated QC if they qualify. At the Old Bailey (preferred to Central Criminal Court), the Recorder of London and the Common Serjeant are full-time judges.

Refer to the Recorder of London, Sir John Smith QC, or the Recorder of London. Judge John Smith, as appropriate. The Common Serjeant, Judge John Smith. Later references to the Recorder (cap) or the Common Serjeant or the judge.

High Court: the High Court sits at the Law Courts (often called the Royal Courts of Justice) in London and in some provincial cities. Refer to a High Court hearing in Manchester. The High Court contains three divisions:

Chancery Division: day-to-day work is conducted by the Chancellor of the Chancery Division and High Court judges. "The Chancellor, Sir John Smith, said at a High Court hearing in London." For other judges: Mr Justice Smith or, later, the judge.

Queen's Bench Division: the Lord Chief Justice, Lord Smith, later Lord Smith or the Lord Chief Justice. For other judges: Mr Justice Smith, later refer to the judge.

Family Division: the President of the Family Division of the High Court, Sir John Smith (or Lord Smith). Later references to the President or Sir John (or Lord Smith). Other judges: Mr Justice Smith or, later, the judge.

Supreme Court: final court of appeal for England, Wales and Northern Ireland, and, in civil cases only, for Scotland.

When sitting as a court, it consists of the Justices of the Supreme Court in Ordinary, who are life peers, and peers of Parliament who have held high judicial office. These were previously known as the Law Lords.

Superior courts other than the Court of Appeal hear some appeals. The Lord Chief Justice, Lords Justices of Appeal and judges of the Queen's Bench Division sit in the Court of Appeal, Criminal and Civil Divisions. When more than one judge takes part in a case, name them all.

Youth courts: refer to Sometown youth court and to John Smith, the chairman. It is illegal to publish the name, address, school or any particulars leading to the identification of any youth who is involved in the proceedings, even as a witness or complainant.

Youth courts deal with people under 17 who may, however, appear, in certain circumstances, before adult courts.

Restrictions on identification apply to youths in adult courts only if the judge so orders.

Even if no order is made it is usual to name youths only in serious cases. In reports from youth courts use "accused of" not "charged with", and avoid the words "convicted" and "convictions".

Magistrates' courts: Sometown magistrates' court (plural possessive even when a case is heard by a single magistrate).

The sitting magistrates are also known as the Bench.

District Judge John Smith; John Smith, the district judge.

REPORTING RESTRICTIONS

The law imposes strict restrictions on reports of committal proceedings, preparatory hearings (Crown Court) in serious fraud cases, divorce and matrimonial cases and certain sex cases.

Courts also have power to order the postponement of the reporting of a case while there is danger of it causing prejudice, usually when people are tried separately on charges arising from the same incident or where the accused is also a defendant in other proceedings.

Reports of committals for trial and hearings preliminary to them are limited to the name of the court and magistrates, names, addresses and occupations of parties and witnesses and the ages of defendants and witnesses, offences charged or, a summary of them, names of lawyers, the decision of the court, the charges on which a person is committed or a summary, the court to which he is committed, the date and place of any adjournment, arrangement as to bail, whether legal aid was granted, any decision to lift or refuse to lift the restrictions.

The restrictions do not apply if the accused person applies to have them lifted, the magistrates decide not to commit, or the court decides to deal with the case summarily.

If the court commits some people and tries others summarily, evidence relevant to those dealt with summarily may be reported. If one or more of the accused wants the restrictions lifted and others want them to stay, the court gives a ruling.

Reports from divorce courts and magistrates' court matrimonial hearings may contain only names, addresses and occupations of the parties and witnesses, a concise statement of the charges, defence and counter-charges on which evidence has been given, submissions and decisions on points of law, the judgment and any observations of the court.

Even when there is no legal prohibition, complainants in other sex cases should be identified only after reference to the news desk or senior production staff.

SCOTTISH COURTS

Scotland has its own system of law and its own courts. Procedure differs greatly from that of English and Welsh courts.

Traditionally Scottish judges have been sterner in their view of contempt than their English counterparts, although the 1981 Contempt of Court Act covers the whole of the United Kingdom.

Under the Criminal Procedure (Scotland) Act 1995, it is an offence to publish any information leading to the identification of any children under 16 involved in criminal proceedings whether they are accused, witnesses or victims (unless the person under 16 is involved as a witness only and no one against whom the proceedings are taken is under 16).

Justice of the Peace Court

This is a lay court where a Justice of the Peace who is not legally qualified sits with a legally qualified clerk. The clerk provides advice to the Justices on matters of law and procedure. The maximum sentence that a JP may impose is 60 days' imprisonment or a fine not exceeding £2,500. In Glasgow only, some courts are presided over by a legally qualified stipendiary magistrate. The maximum sentence that a stipendiary magistrate may impose is 12 months' imprisonment or a fine not exceeding £10,000.

Justice of the Peace Courts replaced former District Courts which were operated by local authorities.

Sheriff courts

Each of Scotland's six sheriffdoms has a sheriff principal and they are divided into sheriff court districts. Courts are presided over by sheriffs who sometimes sit with a jury and may also hear civil cases. Scotburgh sheriff court. The sheriff, Mr Ian McSmith.

High Court of Justiciary

The High Court of Justiciary is Scotland's supreme criminal court. It has jurisdiction over the whole of Scotland and over all crimes. When exercising its appellate jurisdiction it sits only in Edinburgh. The only further appeal possible is to the Supreme Court.

All Scottish judges (there are currently 33) can hear cases (see Court of Session).

Prosecutions may be conducted by the Lord Advocate or the Solicitor General but normally by Crown counsel referred to as advocates depute.

Appeals in serious cases are heard by three judges or more of the High Court.

When sitting as an appeal court, the court consists of at least three judges when hearing appeals against conviction and two when hearing sentence appeals. More judges may sit when the court is dealing with exceptionally difficult cases or those where important matters of law may be considered. Appeals are heard from the High Court, the Sheriff Courts and the District Courts. The High Court also hears appeals in cases referred to it by the Scottish Criminal Cases Review Commission. Refer as appropriate to the Scottish High Court sitting in xxxx, a Scottish appeal court sitting in xxxx.

Civil cases may be heard in sheriff courts or the Court of Session. The Court of Session, the superior civil court, is divided into the Outer House and the Inner House.

The Outer House has (currently 22) judges called Lords Ordinary, who sit alone or with juries. The Inner House has two divisions. In the first division the Lord President presides over four judges (three make a quorum). The Lord Justice Clerk presides in the second division.

Court of Session judges also make up the High Court which hears serious criminal cases. In criminal cases, the Lord President is referred to as the Lord Justice General. Refer to The Lord President, Lord McSmith; the Lord Justice General, Lord McSmith; the Lord Justice Clerk, Lord McSmith; or, for other judges, to the judge or Lord McSmith.

Terms found in Scottish court stories include:

Advocate, equivalent to an English barrister who used to enjoy exclusive right of audience in higher courts.

Solicitor-Advocate, member of the Law Society of Scotland. An experienced solicitor who obtains an extension of their rights of audience in the lower courts by undergoing additional training.

Crown Office, roughly equivalent to the Department of the Director of Public Prosecutions.

Defender (not defendant) in civil cases.

Depute (not deputy) in legal titles.

Interdict is the equivalent of an injunction.

Not proven. Although this verdict differs from a finding of not guilty, the accused person cannot be tried again on the same criminal charge. However, a subsequent civil claim for damages by the victim's family may be brought.

Pursuer or petitioner (according to the procedure adopted) is a claimant.

Procurator fiscal investigates and prosecutes crime in the sheriff court districts under the supervision of the Crown Office. He can give general directions to the police and decides whether an accused person should be held in custody or released until his trial, or whether the case should continue. The procurator fiscal questions an accused person at a private hearing by a sheriff before whom the accused must appear within 24 hours of arrest (48 hours at weekends). Refer to Ian McSmith, procurator fiscal.

EUROPEAN COURTS

European Court of Justice deals with European Union law. Its decisions are binding on British courts. Do not confuse with the European Court of Human Rights. However, please note that the provisions of the European Convention on Human

Rights are incorporated into UK law by the Human Rights Act 1998. Our courts therefore have to bear these provisions in mind when making a decision, particularly in the areas of privacy and libel.

PRIVY COUNCIL

Privy Council: the judicial committee of the Privy Council is the supreme court of appeal for some Commonwealth countries and also hears appeals from some professional disciplinary bodies and Church sources. It consists of three or five senior judges, usually Justices of the Supreme Court or senior Commonwealth judges.

Order in Council: this refers to a ruling by the Privy Council and should be capitalised.

A member of the Privy Council is a Privy Counsellor.

CONSISTORY COURTS

Consistory courts, which are the courts of the established Church, exist in each diocese of the Church of England. In the Diocese of Canterbury it is known as the Commissary Court. They deal with matters affecting churchyards, church property, and try clergy below the rank of bishop who are accused of improper or immoral acts under the Clergy Discipline Act of 1892.

They are presided over by a canon lawyer called the Chancellor (in the Canterbury diocese the Commissary-General). The court of appeal for matters of doctrine, ceremonial or ritual is the Court for Ecclesiastical Causes Reserved; for all other matters it is the Arches Court for the Province of Canterbury and the Chancery Court for the Province of York.

PLACES AND PEOPLES

'They may look sweet, but if you call
one an eskimo he'll bite your head off'

Use the Gazetteer for checking British place names, hyphenation, etc at **www.gazetteer.co.uk**

Britons not Britishers or Brits except in quotations, Great Britain includes England, Scotland and Wales.

Normally write about Britain or, when there is an Irish angle to the story, to mainland Britain. The United Kingdom or the abbreviation UK is to be avoided whether as a noun or an adjective unless the story has a specific relevance to Northern Ireland that would make the use of "Britain" or "British" wrong.

Local and regional government in Britain has been complicated by the 1995 recommendations of the Local Government Commission, mostly approved by the secretary of state in 1996. These reduced the number of shire counties and created almost 50 unitary authorities in England.

In addition there are metropolitan district councils and district councils and, in Scotland, regional district councils.

Counties in England: Bedfordshire; Buckinghamshire; Cambridgeshire; Cheshire; Cornwall; Cumbria; Derbyshire; Devon; Dorset; Co Durham; East Sussex; Essex; Gloucestershire; Hampshire; Herefordshire; Hertfordshire; Kent; Lancashire; Leicestershire; Lincolnshire; Norfolk; Northamptonshire; Northumberland; North Yorkshire; Nottinghamshire; Oxfordshire; Shropshire; Somerset; Staffordshire; Suffolk; Surrey; Warwickshire; West Sussex; Wiltshire; Worcestershire.

Abbreviations in lists and addresses: Beds, Berks, Bucks, Cambs, Glos, Hants, Herts, Lancs, Leics, Lincs, Northants, Notts, Oxon, Staffs, Wilts. Use Devon (not Devonshire). Co Durham, East Sussex, West Sussex, North Yorkshire (N Yorks in lists and addresses) need all their caps to show that they are independent counties. Salop is no longer acceptable for Shropshire.

Use caps for **regions:** the North, the North East (no hyphen in any region), West Country, East Anglia, but eastern England. East Midlands, West Midlands and ceremonial counties East, West and South Yorkshire, but eastern England, south Devon and north Lancashire, etc.

Newcastle upon Tyne, Newcastle-under-Lyme, St Helens, Merseyside, St Helen's, Isle of Wight.

Isles of Scilly, not the Scillies.

Windermere, not Lake Windermere. In place names mere means lake.

Scotland: the people are Scots, the adjective Scottish, although Scotch can refer to eggs, pies, whisky and wool shops.

Scottish local government authorities: Aberdeen City; Aberdeenshire; Angus; Argyll and Bute; Ayrshire East; Ayrshire North; Ayrshire South; Clackmannanshire; Dumfries and Galloway; Dunbartonshire East; Dunbartonshire West; Dundee City; Edinburgh (City of); Falkirk; Fife; Glasgow (City of); Highland; Inverclyde; Lanarkshire North; Lanarkshire South; Lothian East; Lothian West; Midlothian; Moray; Orkney (not Orkneys); Perth and Kinross; Renfrewshire; Renfrewshire East; Scottish Borders; Shetland (not Shetlands); Stirling; Western Isles.

St Andrews. No possessive.

Wales: the administrative areas are the Isle of Anglesey; Blaenau Gwent; Bridgend; Caerphilly; Cardiff; Ceredigion; Carmarthenshire; Conwy; Denbighshire; Flintshire; Gwynedd; Merthyr Tydfil; Monmouthshire; Neath Port Talbot; Newport; Pembrokeshire; Powys; Rhondda Cynon Taff; Swansea; Torfaen; Vale of Glamorgan; Wrexham.

When there is no style ruling to the contrary, follow spellings in the Municipal Year Book for local government entities.

Ireland includes Northern Ireland and the Republic of Ireland. Irish Government means the one in Dublin. Use Irish Republic or the Republic according to context, but not Eire. Ulster is acceptable for Northern Ireland. Never the Six Counties. Co Down, Co Cork, etc, not County Down, County Cork.

Foreign place names: there is no golden rule and no all-purpose reference book. Unless there is a style ruling follow the Statesman's Year Book or, failing that, the Columbia Lippincott Gazetteer.

Although North, South, East and West take caps for regions of the world or of countries which are regarded as political, economic, cultural or historical entities they remain lower case for sections of continents and countries, unless the name of the country is left understood.

Thus: Far East, but south-east Asia. the East-West political divide, the Deep South, the southern United States, the Midwest (or Middle West), South Africa but southern, north, west or east Africa, Eastern Europe but, these days, east Germany.

Names of geographical features often include words which should not be repeated in translation (Rio Grande, not Rio

Grande river or River Rio Grande; Sierra Nevada, not Sierra Nevada mountains). In Arabic place names, avoid transliterations that have come through French — wadi (dry river bed) not ouadi, jebel (mountain) not djebel, and use Tel (not Tell) for hill. In Egypt, burg (tower), gebel, gisr (bridge), marg (field), instead of burj, jebel, jisr and marj.

Note these spellings and styles:

Aden (capital of the united Yemens is now Sana'a, not Sa'na). Alpine to describe the geographical region, alpine to describe a generic sport.
Altrincham (no G).
American refers to the United States of America unless the context dictates otherwise. Avoid adjectival use of US except in heads or compounds such as US-Russian. North America can be used to refer to the United States and Canada.
American Indians, not native Americans.
Andalusia
Arctic: the Arctic, Arctic Circle, Arctic Ocean, but Arctic current.
Argentina: never The Argentine. The people are Argentines, not Argentinians. The adjective is Argentine, not Argentinian.
Asian or Asians, not Asiatic or Asiatics.

Baghdad
Bahamians (people of the Bahamas).
Bahrain
Banjul, capital of Gambia.

Barbadians

Basle, Switzerland.

Basutho (the people of Lesotho, sing and pl). Adjective is Basotho.

Batswana (people of Botswana, sing, pl and adj).

Bayreuth (Germany).

Beirut (Lebanon).

Beijing not Peking.

Belize (formerly British Honduras). Capital is Belmopan.

Bermudians

Berne

Berwick-upon-Tweed

Bhutan

Bosporus, not Bosphorus or the Bosporus Strait.

Botswana for the country.

Brasilia (capital of Brazil).

Buenos Aires

Burma, but note that it calls itself Myanmar, so explain where necessary.

Cairngorm: ignore the name CairnGorm, as the landscape cannot be rebranded.

Cambodia, Cambodians: explain references to Kampuchea. Khmers are the ethnic group.

Cameroon, not Cameroons, nor Cameroun.

Caribbean

Christchurch (Hants and New Zealand).

City: cap only when part of the official title or in references to the City (financial centre). New York City only when readers may think there is a reference to New York state.

Colombia but British Columbia.

Comoros – not Comoro Islands.

Congo: the Republic of Congo, capital Brazzaville, and the Democratic Republic of Congo, formerly Zaire, capital Kinshasa. Our style is to use the full titles at first reference, then to call the Republic Congo-Brazzaville (as is widely done in Africa) and to call the Democratic Republic "Congo" at subsequent uses.

Continent and Continental take caps only to distinguish "mainland" Europe.

We should remember that Britain is geographically in Europe.

Dakar (Senegal).

Darfur is a region of Sudan, not a province. It is divided into three provinces: Northern Darfur (local capital El Fasher), Southern Darfur (local capital Nyala) and Western Darfur (local capital El Geneina).

Dhaka (Bangladesh).

Dhahran

Djibouti

Dnieper (river),

Dnepropetrovsk,

Dniester (river).

Dominica and the Dominican Republic are not the same. Always clarify.

Dutch (preferred) or Netherlanders but never Hollanders.

Ecuador not Equador.

Eskimos. This is taken by Canadian eskimos as an insult. They should be called Inuit.

Far East: (Burma, Cambodia, China, Hong Kong, Japan, Laos, Malaysia, North and South Korea. Singapore, Taiwan, Thailand, Vietnam). Avoid being specific about boundaries of the region.
French Canadians (no hyphen), but Irish-Americans, German-Americans.
Fujiyama not Mount Fujiyama. Often called Fuji.

Gambia, not The Gambia.
Germanies is the plural for the former East and West Germany.
Guinea: formerly French Guinea; Guinea-Bissau, formerly Portuguese Guinea.
Gulf: not Iranian, nor Persian, nor even Arabian; just The Gulf.
Guyana, formerly British Guiana. Guyanese for the people.

Hague. The Hague takes a cap T.
Hercegovina not Herzegovina.
Hispaniola, the island comprising the Dominican Republic and Haiti.
Holland. Use the Netherlands only in formal political contexts.
Hong Kong

Indo-China/Indo-Chinese: (NOT Indochina).
Indian cities: Mumbai is now accepted use for Bombay, though there may be occasion to use Bombay because of historical connotations, for commercial references, or

quoting somebody. Chennai is now the name Indians use
for Madras, but to clarify write Chennai (formerly Madras)
if it is unclear where we are talking about. Bangalore and
Calcutta thus.
Iran, Iranians. Iraq, Iraqis.
Istanbul: Constantinople only in historical references.
Izmir: Smyrna only in historical references.

Jakarta

Kathmandu
Khartoum
Kilimanjaro, not Mount Kilimanjaro.
Kosovo, not Kosova.

Lesotho. The people and the adjective are Basotho.
Liege (but Liegeois, the Belgian Embassy informs us —
ignore Lippincott).
Livorno, not Leghorn.
Llanelli
Lod (Israel), formerly Lydda.
Luxembourg
Lyon, not Lyons.

Macedonia
Madagascar, not the Malagasy Republic except in quoted
matter. The people (sing and pl) and the adjective are
Malagasy.
Majorca, not Mallorca.
Malaysia is the nation of which Malaya is a part. The people

are Malaysian unless there is a specific reference to the Malays, or preferably, Malayans, as an ethnic group.

Marseille, not Marseilles.

Middle East. Mid-East only in heads. Do not use Near East.

Middlesbrough (not Middlesborough).

Midwest (or Middle West): Indiana, Illinois, Iowa, Kansas, Michigan, Minnesota, Missouri, Nebraska, North Dakota, Ohio, South Dakota and Wisconsin.

Mogadishu (Somalia).

Monaco: the people are Monégasque (s).

N'Djamena is the capital of Chad.

Newcastle upon Tyne (no hyphens).

Neuchatel is in Switzerland, Neufchâtel in France.

Newcastle-under-Lyme

Nigerians come from Nigeria.

Nigerois come from Niger.

Nuremberg

Papua New Guinea (no hyphens).

Pashtu is preferable to Pathan or Pushtu.

Philippines: adjective is Philippine; but adjective for the people, Filipino; Filipina for women.

Phnom Penh

Port-au-Prince (Haiti).

Port of Spain (Trinidad).

Quebecois (people and adjective) only in references to the French Canadian people and culture: though a reference to a female would be Quebecoise.

Riyadh
Romania
Rwanda

Sahara. Sahara Desert is tautological.
Saint John, New Brunswick; St Johns, Quebec; St John's, Newfoundland.
Salzburg
Saudi Arabia: never just Saudi, which is the adjective.
Schiphol: airport outside Amsterdam.

Former Soviet Union: the states (preferable to the term republics, although can be used synonymously) are: Armenia; Azerbaijan – adjective: Azerbaijani for people and state; Belarus – not double s – adjective: Belarussian; Georgia; Kazakhstan – adjective Kazakh (not Kazakhi or Turkmeni, etc); Kyrgyzstan – adjective Kyrgyz; Moldova – Moldovan; Russia or the Russian Federation (synonymous), but not the Russian republic; Tajikistan – Tajik; Turkmenistan (note the i) – Turkmen; Ukraine – (not the Ukraine); but the Crimea; Uzbekistan – Uzbek; also: the Baltic states (not republics), Estonia, Latvia and Lithuania, all now in Nato and the EU; autonomous republic: Tatarstan (not Tataria); Yakutia; Bashkiria; Chechnya; Ingushetia; Nagorno Karabakh (no hyphen); but Alma-Ata. Kishinev, capital of Moldova, not Chisnau; Lvov, not Lviv. Yekaterinburg (formerly Sverdlovsk) must have 'y' at start. Sri Lanka (formerly Ceylon): the people are Sri Lankans, but differentiate when necessary between Sinhalese and Tamils.

St, Ste: Normally abbreviated in place names, but there are exceptions.
Stoke-on-Trent
Stratford-on-Avon district council, but Stratford upon Avon (town).
Sudan (no'the').

Tbilisi (Georgia), formerly Tiflis.
Tehran
Temple Mount: needs occasional Muslim translation, "Temple Mount, known to Muslims as the Noble Sanctuary (Al Haram al Sharif)".

United Arab Emirates. Abbreviate to UAE only when the full title has been used repeatedly; the Emirates. They are: Abu Dhabi, Dubai, Sharja, Ajman, Fujaira, Umm al Qaiwain, Ras al Khaima.
United Kingdom. This includes Northern Ireland. Do not use the phrase interchangeably with Great Britain.
United States. US (no full points) only in heads and in compounds like US-European. Use American as the adjective unless there is danger of confusion with another country in North America or South America.

Valletta
Vienna

Washington. Use DC (for District of Columbia) only when necessary to distinguish from the state of Washington on the Pacific Coast. Washington state or the state of Washington.

West Bank: West Bank of the Jordan, the Jordan West Bank or, when the context is clear, the West Bank.

Yemen: the united former North Yemen and South Yemen. Capital is Sana'a.

Yerevan (Armenia), formerly Erivan.

THE SERVICES

The Royal Navy is the Navy except in formal contexts. Foreign navies, like foreign armies and air forces, are lower case (a Washington official said the navy would ...).

The Royal Marines, the Marines, a marine. The United States Marines but later, American marines.

Acceptable abbreviations of naval ranks and ratings: Adml, Vice-Adml, Rear-Adml, Cdre (Commodore), Capt, Cdr, Lt-Cdr, Lt, Sub-Lt, CPO, Midshipman Warrant Officer PO (for Chief Petty Officer and Petty Officer, only in lists and after first mention), Ldg Seaman, AB. Technical ratings in full. Admiral of the Fleet. Do not write RN after the names of admirals. NB: Field Marshals, Admirals of the Fleet and Marshals of the Royal Air Force never retire.

Submarines should be adequately described: Polaris or Trident submarines (nuclear-powered, armed with nuclear missiles); fleet submarines (nuclear-powered but conventionally armed); patrol submarines (non-nuclear). Patrol submarines are the only submarines referred to as boats.

See Ships in the glossary for terminology.

The Army is capped at every mention, foreign armies only at first mention.

With names write: Field Marshal, Gen, Lt Gen, Maj Gen, Brig, Col, Lt Col, Major (NB: Major is never abbreviated), Capt, Lieut, 2nd Lieut, WO1, WO2, (warrant officers), RSM (Regimental Sergeant Major), CSM (Company Sergeant Major), SSM (Squadron Sergeant Major), BSM (Battery Sergeant Major) – all except the RSM can be termed just Sergeant Major – Sgt, Cpl, L/Cpl, Pte, Gm, Gdmn. Please note Bombardier and Lance Bombardier are ranks used in artillery units instead of Corporal and Lance Corporal.

Abbreviate Driver, Trooper, Rifleman, Gunner (Dvr, Tpr, Rfn, Gnr) only in lists. Do not abbreviate Drum Major, Pipe Major or any ranks or appointments peculiar to one or a few regiments or corps.

Adjutant. CO (commanding officer) is correct only for battalions or regiments. Lower units have an officer commanding or plural officers commanding but do not use OC. Higher units have a commander (e.g. the Brigade Commander, the Divisional Commander, the Corps Commander, the Army Commander). Always abbreviate C-in-C, Cs-in-C, GOC.

Do not confuse Colonel in Chief, an appointment accepted by a (usually royal) notable as a compliment to the regiment, with a lieutenant colonel (or other officer) commanding a battalion (infantry) or regiment (cavalry and artillery units) of the British Army. The Colonel of the Regiment is usually a retired senior officer of the regiment/battalion responsible for recruiting. His is an honorary position. Some regiments have a Colonel Commandant (e.g. the Parachute Regiment, the Gurkhas).

The Household Cavalry and the Foot Guards make up the Household Division; the Foot Guards alone constitute the Guards Division. The Household Cavalry Regiment (HCR) is the only regiment of mounted troops and was formed from the amalgamation of the Blues and Royals and the Life Guards, which still exist within it; there is a Service Regiment of the HCR with armoured cars. The King's Troop, Royal Horse Artillery, wear busbies, unlike guardsmen, who wear bearskins.

Follow these styles for units and formations: 21st Army Group or Northern Army Group. First Army XI Corps (roman numerals), 3rd Division, S Brigade, 1st Bn Royal Regiment of Wales or 1st Royal Regiment of Wales. Spell out company, battery, squadron, platoon.

Corps have a historic order of precedence, now relevant for their place in formations on parades.

Titles and precedence of corps:
1. The Life Guards: the Blues and Royals (forming the Household Cavalry).
2. Royal Horse Artillery (part of Royal Artillery).
3. Royal Armoured Corps (see separate list).

4. Royal Regiment of Artillery (usually Royal Artillery).
5. Corps of Royal Engineers (usually Royal Engineers).
6. Royal Corps of Signals.
7. Regiments of Foot Guards.
8. Regiments of Infantry (see separate list).
9. Special Air Service Regiment (22 SAS is the regular regiment; 21 or 23 TA).
10. Army Air Corps.
11. Royal Army Chaplains' Department.
12. Royal Logistic Corps.
13. Royal Army Medical Corps.
14. Corps of Royal Electrical and Mechanical Engineers.
15. Adjutant General's Corps.
16. Royal Army Veterinary Corps.
17. Small Arms School Corps.
18. Royal Army Dental Corps.
19. Intelligence Corps.
20. Army Physical Training Corps.
21. General Service Corps.
22. Queen Alexandra's Royal Army Nursing Corps.
23. Royal Monmouthshire Royal Engineers (Militia) (Territorial Army).
24. The Honourable Artillery Company (Territorial Army).
25. Territorial Army (other than 23 and 24 above).

Precedence of Foot Guards:
1st Bn Grenadier Guards.
1st Bn Coldstream Guards.
1st Bn Scots Guards.

1st Bn Irish Guards.
1st Bn Welsh Guards.

Precedence of Royal Armoured Corps:
1st The Queen's Dragoon Guards.
The Royal Scots Dragoon Guards (Carabiniers and Greys).
The Royal Dragoon Guards.
The Queen's Royal Hussars (The Queen's Own and Royal Irish).
9th/12th Royal Lancers (Prince of Wales's).
The King's Royal Hussars.
The Light Dragoons.
The Queen's Royal Lancers.
1st Royal Tank Regiment.
2nd Royal Tank Regiment.

Precedence of Infantry Regiments:
1. The Royal Scots (The Royal Regiment).
2. The Princess of Wales's Royal Regiment.
3. The Duke of Lancaster's Regiment.
4. The Royal Regiment of Fusiliers.
5. The Royal Anglian Regiment.
6. The Royal Marines.
7. The Yorkshire Regiment.
8. The Mercian Regiment.
9. The Royal Welsh Regiment.
10. The Royal Irish Regiment.
11. The Parachute Regiment.
12. The Royal Gurkha Rifles.
13. The Rifles.

The Royal Air Force

Prefer the RAF except on formal occasions. Air Force is permitted. Lower case for foreign air forces after first mention.

Marshal of the Royal Air Force, Air Chief Marshal, Air Marshal, Air Vice-Marshal (MRAF, Air Chf Mshl, Air Mshl, AVM in lists or when there are repeated references) Air Cdre, Gp Capt, Wg Cdr, Sqn Ldr, Flt Lt, Fg Off, Plt Off, Warrant Officer, Flight Sergeant, Chief Technician (WO, FS, Ch Tech only for lists or repeated references), Sgt, Cpl, Jnr Tech, SAC Tech, LAC, AC.

The rank is aircraftman, even if he is a craftsman.

Courts martial. Their findings and sentences are subject to confirmation and this should always be pointed out. Cashiering is far more serious than mere dismissal; do not confuse. A naval officer may be dismissed his ship (not dismissed from his ship).

POLITICS

The Houses of Parliament; Parliament, but in this parliament (describing a particular term); parliamentary (the parliamentary Labour Party); House of Lords, the House of Commons, the Lords, the Commons, the Chamber. The Speaker, James Smith, the Leader of the Opposition.

The pre-legistative process may begin with a Green Paper, which is a discussion document, or a White Paper, which contains firm proposals.

Before becoming Acts, Bills have first, second and third readings and pass the report and committee stages before receiving the Royal Assent. Front bench (group of leaders), front-bench (adj), frontbencher, back benches, back-bench (adj), backbenchers. He took his seat on the front bench. Private member's Bill.

Party names for debates and lists: Conservative (C), Labour (Lab), Liberal Democrat (Lib Dem), Scottish National Party (SNP), Plaid Cymru (PC or Welsh Nationalist), Social Democratic and Labour Party (SDLP), Ulster Unionist (UU), Democratic Unionist Party (DUP), United Ulster Unionist (UUU), British National Party (BNP), Communist Party (Comm), Socialist Workers' Party (SWP).

Tory is acceptable as a synonym for Conservative; Socialist is no longer acceptable as a synonym for Labour. New Labour is acceptable to describe the recent incarnation of the party, but old labour. Sects within parties are capped; the Tory Reform Group, the Militant Tendency, the Bow Group. Lib Dem is fine for Liberal Democrat.

Ministers: the Secretary of State for Defence, the Defence Secretary, the Minister for Schools, the Schools Minister.

Reports of the deaths or retirements of MPs should always be followed by a footnote giving the result in the constituency at the last general election and any relevant by-election. The style is: general election or 2010 by-election Sometown East: J Smith (C) 50,000; W Brown (Lab) 40,000. C maj 10,000.

The Government, but government spokesmen: the Opposition but opposition policies. A select committee, the select committee on transport: the standing committee on whatever.

Rt Hon does not need to be spelt out in full, even within quotations.

When writing about departments of State verify the correct title. There can be difficulties with prepositions, and titles often change at reshuffles. Note, for example, that it is the Department of Health, but the Department for Transport.

The old rule about capping general election only when we meant the current one, and lowercasing the words when we meant the last, the next, or any previous one, was confusing. Use lower case.

Under devolution, Scotland does not have a government it has an executive. It may also be referred to as the devolved administration. Members of the Scottish Executive should be referred to as ministers rather than secretaries. Refer to the Scottish Parliament, the Welsh Assembly and the Northern Ireland Assembly. The administrations in those places are led by a First Minister.

European Union: the EU is the collective term following the Maastricht Treaty. It does not include the European Court of Human Rights, which is part of a separate body. The EU includes the three "pillars" of the Union which are:

The EC (formerly the European Economic Community, renamed the EC by Maastricht) which includes the Council of Ministers, European Court of Justice, European Commission and the European Parliament. The EC is the machine which drives through and implements directives and regulations through these institutions.

The other two "inter-governmental pillars" are common foreign and security policy, and justice and home affairs. These were also created at Maastricht. Governments of the member states have agreed to co-operate in these areas but policy is not driven through the EC institutions. It is agreed by co-operation outside the EC institutional framework.

Therefore
The EU is the correct "club" name. It includes the EC and the two other pillars. It is right to use EU as a collective term. "The EU decided this", "EU member-states did that".

The EC is the core of the Union. It manages the single market and other areas such as competition but does not have power to initiate and push through legislation in areas that fall under the "inter-governmental pillars". If you are referring to a directive it could either be called an EC directive or an EU directive, but EC would be more correct.

The commission is part of the EC. It is run by 27 commissioners appointed by member governments and initiates legislation. It is wrong to use EC when referring to the commission. The commission has to be called either the commission or, to avoid repetition, "Brussels".

European Parliament: Euro-MP, member of the European Parliament. MEP is also acceptable.

NUMBERS, MEASURES AND MONEY

Spell out numbers below 10: one, nine, first, fourth, 17th, 123rd, 999. One million, two million, 10 million, 999 million. Give broken millions in full only when it is misleading to decimalise to two places; 2,736,123 but prefer 2.74 million. One billion (= 1,000 million), two billion, 25 billion. Avoid using billion if only one or two figures in a series exceed 999 million; then write, say, 1,345 million. Avoid trillion (= million million) if possible.

Use a thin space to separate a numeral and a word when they are part of the same number e.g. £2 million.

Use figures at all times with currency signs and abbreviations: £1, $2. Abbreviate million to m and billion to bn in headlines. No spaces needed to separate the number and letter.

In stories concerned mainly with money, company reports and City page references to bids and deals, use m and bn. In news stories as distinct from stories in the business section always write million and billion in full.

Decimal points: these appear at the bottom of numbers, not halfway up them.

Money: 1p, 99p, £1, £1.33. Only pounds, United States dollars and the euro take symbols in general news and feature copy. All other currencies are anglicised: first mention Swiss francs, Canadian dollars, Turkish lire and so on, then, francs, dollars, etc.

In lists on City pages and when it has been established which currency is being referred to, these abbreviations may be used: Australia A$, Canada C$, Hong Kong HK$, India Rs, Israel Shl, Japan Y, Saudi Arabia SR, South Africa R, Switzerland Sfr. The plural of lira is lire. Sweden has the krona (Skr) with the plural kronor, Norway the krone (Nkr) with the plural kroner, and Denmark the krone (Dkr) with the plural kroner.

Give sterling equivalents in brackets after references to foreign currencies. If writing a story that includes reference to the pre-decimal coinage, use the following abbreviations: £ for pound, s for shilling and d for pence as in £7 15s 6d. There were four farthings in a penny, 12 pence in a shilling and 20 shillings in a pound, 21 shillings in a guinea. A 2s piece was a florin, a 2s 6d piece a half-crown, and there were five shillings in a crown.

Use common British weights and measures even in foreign stories unless the context dictates otherwise. Metric weights and measures should be followed by British equivalents in brackets. Use the abbreviations oz, lb, st, cwt, in, ft, yd after numerals from two upwards. No full points, no plurals, no space between the number and the abbreviation.

Do not abbreviate acres, miles, pints, gallons. One pound, less than a hundredweight, a few ounces, 7lb, 5st, lost 5lb, 5lb 7oz. Two miles, 27 miles, two acres, 125 acres, 2ft, 2ft 3in, 3yd, 3yd 2ft, two square yards, 22 sq yd.

Usually it is not necessary to distinguish between the ton (imperial, 2,240lb) and the tonne (metric ton of 1,000 kilograms = 2,204.6lb). Use tons unless the small difference is important.

Financial years and other periods of time should be rendered with a hyphen, not a slash, e.g. 2006-07.

Fractions: Use half, quarter, three quarters, third, fifth, eighth in preference to decimals in general copy. Use decimals when they aid comprehension or comparison, but not with imperial measurements: e.g. write 3ft 9in rather than 3.75 feet, or 6lb 8oz not 6.5lb. Do not use decimals and fractions in the same story except when necessary in financial copy. In money markets all dealings are in fractions. Write 2, but one-quarter per cent.

If it is necessary to use oddities such as two one-hundredths of a second, ensure that the use of the hyphen and the word "one" prevents confusion with two hundredths. Two 100ths of a second or 200th of a second are ugly, but may be necessary.

Percentages: per cent does not take a full point. Use pc only in headlines and % only in tables. In City page copy pc is acceptable. Percentages may be written in numbers — e.g. 5 per cent — if a story contains several of them.

Note the difference between percentages and percentage points. If interest rates rise from 10 to 11 per cent, the increase is one percentage point or 10 per cent.

Metric units should not be abbreviated at first mention, except for mm for the calibre of weapons and the size of film. Litre should always be written in full, except in lists. The metric system is based on the metre (abbreviation is m), the litre (l) and the gram (g), and uses prefixes to denote that the unit has been divided or multiplied.

The prefixes are (with abbreviations): deca (da) multiplied by 10, as in decagram meaning 10 grams; hecto or hect (h) multiplied by 100; kilo (k) multiplied by 1,000; mega (M) multiplied by a million. Deci (d) means tenth, centi (c) a hundredth, as in cl = hundredth of a litre; milli (m) a thousandth.

Common metric measures with abbreviations and equivalents include:

Millimetre (mm) 0.039in, centimetre (cm) 0.394in, metre (m) 1.094yd, kilometre (km) 0.6214 mile, litre (l) 1.76 pints, kilogram (kg) 2.205lb.

When converting approximate distances treat the kilometre as five-eighths of a mile. Multiply centimetres by 0.4 to give inches, metres by 3.3 to give feet, sq metres by 1.2 to give sq yards, cubic metres by 1.31 to give cubic yards.

When in doubt consult the appendix in the *Concise Oxford Dictionary*.

Earthquakes The Richter scale is no longer the most commonly used calibration for earthquakes. Be clear whether the scale used in copy is the Moment scale of magnitude (MMS) or – in historical references – Richter.

Temperatures Raised zeros are omitted in temperatures. The abbreviations F and C indicate degrees. Give Fahrenheit figures followed by Celsius (now preferred to centigrade) in this style: 60F (16C). Temperatures rise by 15 degrees; they do not get warmer by 15 degrees.

To convert from Fahrenheit to Celsius: subtract 32 from the F figure, divide by 9 and multiply by 5.

To convert from Celsius to Fahrenheit: multiply the C figure by 9, divide by 5 then add 32.

GLOSSARY

STATIONERY TRAFFIC

A

a/an: an hour, heir; a hotel, historian (if the h is pronounced, use a).

abdicate, abnegate and abrogate all have different meanings. The first is to renounce high responsibilities; the second to deny oneself or someone else something; the third to abolish by an official proclamation. See also prevaricate.

Aborigine: note the cap A. Aboriginal in its specific use to describe the native Australian people, should also be capped.

accents: accents should be used on all foreign proper names (including anglicised names taking an accent – e.g. John Le Carré) and on some foreign words that have passed into regular English usage. (Be guided by the *Oxford English Dictionary*.) If quoting a foreign phrase that includes a word with an accent, use it. Avoid accents in headlines: they do not need to be used on capital letters (see also italics). The outlandishness of the accent should be limited only by the glyphs available.

accessary for a person (after the fact, for example); accessory for a thing.

Achilles' heel

acid house parties

Act (law) takes a cap at every mention. So does a parliamentary Bill.

actress is the term we use for a female actor.

AD precedes the year (AD 1066). It follows centuries (fourth century AD), although centuries are assumed to be AD unless BC is used.

Addenbrooke's hospital

addresses: the point of giving an address is usually to give the reader an idea of relative geography. If the person concerned lives in a small town it is sufficient to name that town and its county. In the case of a village it should be related to the nearest well-known town. If he or she lives in a large town or city use district names rather than boroughs or postal numbers. Do not presume that people outside London know where, for example, Eltham is. If it is impossible to clarify in an indirect reference, use Eltham, south-east London. Do not give house numbers or names unless there is a compelling reason or the address is famous or notorious (10 Downing Street, 10 Rillington Place). The words Street, Road, Avenue, etc are printed in full and capped.

adjectives. Distinguish between those that are objective, and may be used in news stories - literally descriptive words such as long, short, dark, bumpy, smooth, etc - and those that are subjective and should be avoided - stupid, ugly, craven, brilliant and so on.

adjournment line: in court cases this is now "The case/trial/hearing continues".

adrenalin has no "e" on the end.

adultery requires one party to be married. Anything else is merely fornication.

adverbs are the necessary accompaniment of verbs. One does not do something quick, one does it quickly; one does not sell something cheap, one sells it cheaply; and so on.

advertisement, never ad. Advert is allowed when essential in heads.

adviser but advisory.

Aertex: trade name.

AEW (Airborne Early Warning) but Awacs (Airborne Warning and Control System). In full or with explanation at first mention.

Afrikaner for the people and culture; Afrikaans for the language.

ageing/ageist: not aging/agist.

Agence France Presse

ages: John Smith, 25, not John Smith, aged 25, but 25-year-old John Smith or John Smith, who is 25, are more appealing in narratives or descriptive writing. Avoid Mary Smith, nine, and John Smith, two months. Whereas the adjectival usage is "25-year-old John Smith", the nominal usage is "John Smith, a 25 year-old". The 25 year-old.

Aids: initial cap only. Since it is a condition rather than a disease, write "died of an Aids-related condition", not "died of Aids".

aircraft, which covers helicopters and airships, is the preferred usage, but planes is acceptable in headlines. Where possible be precise: airliner, fighter, trainer. Aircraft types: BAe-III, DC-10, F-III, F-5E, Tu-144, MiG-21. But Boeing 727, Boeing 747-400. The use of hyphens between letters and figures is needed for consistency, although the use of hyphens by manufacturers follows no set pattern. Tornado becomes Tornados in the plural; the cap differentiates the name from the wind and enables us to follow RAF style. Concorde.

Airfix: trade name.

Albany, Piccadilly, not The Albany.

A-level: lc l.

alibi is not an excuse; it means proof of being elsewhere.

Alitalia

al-Jamaa al-Islamiyya: Egyptian terrorist group.

alleged is not a magic incantation against libel and contempt of court. It means said or claimed, but, because of its criminal connotations, can be unfair when used in reporting controversies. Alleged and kindred words are often redundant as in "Police charged him with allegedly murdering ..."

alleluia: not hallelujah.

allies and allied take caps only in established contemporary usages such as Allied Forces, in historical usage (the Allied Powers) or in titles (Supreme Headquarters Allied Powers in Europe, which is normally abbreviated to Shape). The Nato allies, Britain's allies.

all-time high: see tautology. Avoid.

allude to: it means to speak of something without mentioning it directly.

al-Qaeda

alright is an abomination. It is all right.

Alsatian: cap people and dogs.

alternatives: there can only ever be two. Where there is a choice of three or more, they are options.

alumnus/alumni; alumna/alumnae – the singular and plural for men and women who are former members of an educational establishment.

amaze, amazing: avoid.

Americanisms. Do not use an Americanism when there is a reasonable word of our own: i.e. candidates "stand" for office, they do not "run". But "running mate" is permitted in American election stories. American courts do not contain witness boxes, so witness stand is acceptable in reports of American trials.

People live "in" not "on" a street. "Movie" is allowed in stories about the US industry ... otherwise use "film". We do things "at" the weekend, not "on" it.

America's Cup

amok: no *Daily Telegraph* style book would be complete without the observation that only Malays can run amok. See also berserk.

ancestor: an earlier generation of a family. The opposite is descendant.

Andrews liver salts: St Andrews University.

anger: use sparingly in copy, as in life.

angler/fisherman: the difference between the pleasure fisherman and the professional is worth pointing out when writing about people missing off the coast. In one case we may be talking about two men in a dinghy and in the other about an ocean-going trawler.

animals: these are neuter even if we are well aware of their gender. Anthropomorphism has no place in balanced news reporting.

annex: verb.

annexe: noun.

anonymous quotes: under the parliamentary lobby system these are, regrettably, sometimes inevitable. In other circumstances they should be avoided wherever possible.

An Phoblacht: Sinn Fein/IRA newspaper.

anticipate is not a synonym for expect; it conveys the meaning of acting in expectation of an event. A reporter who expects to be sent to Africa may anticipate the assignment by buying tropical clothes. A couple who anticipate marriage may, for instance, open a joint bank account.

any more/anymore: we do not want any more errors in the newspaper; we will not put up with this anymore.

apostrophes should not be used in shortened words that have ceased to be regarded as slang or informal such as "flu" and "cello". "Phone" is acceptable for headlines but keep "telephone" in text. The apostrophe is used to indicate the omission of letters, and in plural forms of lower case letters standing alone (crossing the i's and dotting the t's).

apparatchik

appeal, as a verb, requires the preposition "against": only Americans appeal verdicts and sentences; we appeal against them.

Apple (Macintosh)

aqueduct, not aquaduct.

Aran: one r for knitwear.

arc lamps: outmoded. Use TV lights, floodlights, searchlights, as appropriate.

archaeology

Argentina: Argentine for the citizen and the adjective, not Argentinian.

Argyle: knitwear.

Argyll: the county.

Armageddon

Armed Forces: uc if British.

artefact, not artifact.

arts: to protect the newspaper and website, criticism should refer to the performance rather than the performer. It is safer to say that, on a particular night, an actor did not display the qualities demanded by a role than to say that he is incapable of playing it. Comment must be fair – not inspired by malice – and "on a matter of public interest", which means that discussion of the subject benefits the public, not merely that it satisfies curiosity. Critics and reviewers have as much right as anyone else to express honestly held opinions – but no more. In law no additional rights are conferred on them because they are invited to attend performances or receive books "for favour of review". Conversely the freedom to comment is not restricted by the lack of free tickets.

as is a gloriously imprecise preposition that can mean 'when', 'because' or 'since'. Use any of these three in preference.

ASB: Alternative Service Book.

Asperger's syndrome

Asprey: the jewellers.

assume in an abstract sense is to take something for granted, presume is to make a supposition on the basis of probability.

assure lives, insure property.

as to, as in "as to what", "as to which", is pointless and is banned.

astrology/astronomy — the difference between what is written in the stars and studying them for scientific purpose.

at a point or a village, in an area, town or city.

Attorney General: no hyphen.

autarchy: absolute sovereignty.

autarky: self-sufficiency.

author is a noun. The American habit of using it as a verb is to be studiously avoided.

Ayatollah Khomenei (dead), Khamenei (living).

Aykroyd, Dan

axe: this is an implement used for chopping wood and a weapon of choice for certain murderers. It is not a verb.

While the usage may just about be tolerated in headlines, bear in mind that if someone is axed they have been sacked, if spending is axed it has been cut and if a television programme is axed it is dropped. Ask always whether a violent metaphor is appropriate and in good taste.

B

Ba'ath party

back benches, backbenchers, back-bench (adj).

bacteria: plural form of bacterium.

bale is something made of hay; bail is on a set of cricket stumps or a surety. Bail out is the verbal form, bail-out the noun.

balk/baulk: reserve baulk for snooker; balk otherwise.

balls: unless a ball has an adjective before it (May ball, hunt ball, etc), the plural is "dances".

banister

Ban Ki-moon is at second and subsequent mentions Mr Ban.

Bank of England; the Bank. And it has a Governor, upper case.

Bank Rate – note caps; not base rate (of interest).

Bannister, Sir Roger

Barabbas

barbecue: not barbeque.

Barclays Bank

Barnardo's: note the apostrophe.

baronets: Sir John Smith, Bt, when necessary to distinguish from a knight, but a reference such as "Sir John, the seventh baronet" is often better. Baronets are not knights so never describe them as such.

Barons Court: no apostrophe.

Bartók: note accent.

Baton: a short stick used by the conductor of an orchestra. Batten — a strip of wood. To batten down the hatches means, literally, to secure the hatches of a ship in preparation for bad weather. Metaphorically, it means to prepare for a crisis.

battles: specific ones are capped — the Battle of Hastings, the Battle of Britain.

BBC One, BBC Two for television. BBC Radio 4. See brands.

BC follows dates.

Beaufort scale: index of wind strengths. 1, light air; 2, light breeze; 3, gentle breeze; 4, moderate breeze; 5, fresh breeze; 6, strong breeze; 7, near-gale; 8, gale; 9, strong gale; 10, storm; 11, violent storm; 12, hurricane.

Becher's Brook

Beck's beer

begging the question: a logical fallacy of founding a conclusion on a basis that itself needs to be proved. It does not mean avoiding the question or inviting it. Also known as *petitio principii*. For example: men are awful because they lie. This assumes they do lie, hence it begs the question.

benefited: one t.

Bennet: one t, *Pride and Prejudice*.

Bennett, Alan

Beretta, the gun: not to be confused with biretta.

berserk: no *Daily Telegraph* style book would be complete without the observation that only Icelanders can go berserk. See also amok.

Berwick-upon-Tweed

Beverly Hills

Bible: cap unless figurative (the style book was his bible), biblical. The Bible does not need italicising; nor does the Book of Common Prayer. The Prayer Book is an acceptable form. Bible belt.

biblical references: thus, Genesis 1: 1, Matthew 3: 2.

bid does not mean attempt, even in headlines. Try to use "try" more often.

bi, meaning twice, is best avoided, but, if necessary, use bimonthly, biweekly, biannual. Will the readers know whether you mean twice weekly or every two weeks?

biennial is once every two years: biannual is twice a year.

billion is a thousand million. In the business pages and in headlines it may be abbreviated to bn. Elsewhere in the newspaper and website it must always be written out in full.

Birds Eye is the frozen food (no apostrophe).

biretta: a priest's headgear, not to be confused with beretta (see above).

Biro is a trademark.

Birtwistle, Sir Harrison, has no "h" in his surname.

black is the correct way to refer to those of Afro-Caribbean ethnicity. Capitalise only in titles of organisations. Except in quotations, do not use as a catch-all word for non-white people. Coloured means South African of mixed race; it is always capped and should be explained.

BlackBerry, plural BlackBerrys.

Blanchett, Cate

Bleasdale, Alan

blizzard: do not use lightly for heavy snow. The wind must be at least 35 mph.

bloc as in former Eastern bloc (lc). From the French for a combination of parties or nations formed to achieve a common purpose.

blog is to be preferred to weblog. It refers to a website that publishes entries in reverse chronological order and that usually allows readers to comment on each entry. An individual entry on a blog is a blog post; posts are not comments, which are observations left on a blog by a reader or even by the blogger himself.

blooms are not to be used for flowers.

Blumenthal, Heston

Blu-Tack

Boadicea, not Boudicca.

bolognese sauce does not take a cap. A small amount of chicken liver gives it a nice kick.

Bombay/Mumbai. Mumbai has become accepted use.

Bonhams, the auctioneers.

Bonham Carter, Helena and others: no hyphen.

Bonington, Sir Chris: one "n".

bon viveur is bad French: if you have to use such a term, say *bon vivant.* A woman is a *bonne vivante.*

Boots

Bored with, not bored of.

born of, not born out of.

Botox – botulinum toxin.

bottle bank

bought and brought – The past participles of buy and bring.

bouquet of flowers is a tautology.

Bournville (no middle "e").

Boutros Boutros Ghali: former UN secretary-general.

Boy's Own Paper

BP: no full stops, formerly British Petroleum.

brainchild is a tabloid way of saying idea.

branded: for cattle or specific goods only. Not to be used as a verb to mark someone or something as having a particularly shameful quality. (See dubbed.)

brands: if in doubt about the rendering of a company name — e.g. BlackBerry, easyJet — use the version on its own website.

brave is an acceptable adjective to apply to somebody who has perpetrated a courageous act. Its usage to describe the demeanour of somebody suffering from a serious illness is tabloid.

Breugel. Pieter Breugel the Elder was the most famous member of the family and only one to sign his name without the h (Breughel).

Bridge on the River Kwai requires the definite article: *The Bridge on the River Kwai*. See IMDb.co.uk

brilliant: its legitimate usage to describe a dazzling object is acceptable. Use carefully to describe someone of rare intellectual attainment. Its casual use as an adjective to describe any person or object that we might wish to refer to favourably is ineffably tabloid and is to be avoided.

Brink's-Mat

British Isles: see United Kingdom.

Brooks's Club

Bros only in the official names of companies. No full point.

brussels sprouts

BSE – bovine spongiform encephalopathy (all lc).

BT, no full stops, formerly British Telecom.

bubbly: hackneyed as a description of a lively female, vulgar as the name of a drink. In the second case, use champagne.

Buck's fizz (the drink).

Budget is capped for the Chancellor's statement or foreign equivalents; company or local authority budgets are lower case. But pre-Budget statement.

budget airline is tabloid. Use low-cost.

Buffett, Warren – successful investor also colloquially known as the Sage of Omaha. Buffett has two f's and two t's.

bull: a male bovine; bullock – a bull that has been castrated.

Bulow, Claus von

bumf: NOT bumph (it is short for bum-fodder).

bungee jumping

bureaus not bureaux.

burka, not burqa. Other items of female Muslim dress include the hijab, niqab and chador.

Burns Night: no apostrophe needed.

bused, busing: try to avoid in references to transport. Taken by bus is more elegant. Bussing means kissing.

Bussell, Darcey

bus stop

Buthelezi, Mangosuthu, president of Inkatha.

Butlins: note, no apostrophe.

buy-out/buy out: noun hyphenated; verb two words.

buzzwords

by-election, but bypass and bylaw. Not bye.

C

Cabinet is capped when referring to the British one, not otherwise.

cache/cachet – a hiding place for ammunition and other things. Something conferring status.

caesarean section, not caesarian, lc (like wellington boot). Also: Shakespearean, not Shakespearian.

Cage, Nicolas

Cambodia, not Kampuchea.

Cambridge, the Duke and Duchess of. Formerly known as Prince William and Catherine Middleton.

Cameron, David – the Prime Minister is married to Samantha, and has three children Nancy, Elwen and Florence. His eldest child, Ivan, died in 2009 aged six.

Campaign to Protect Rural England (CPRE).

Campbell, Alastair

Canute: remember that King Canute did not believe that he could turn back the tide. His courtiers had flattered him that he could and his demonstration was to prove them wrong. Therefore, beware of using his name to illustrate folly or bombast.

canvass: to seek views. Canvas for painters.

capping up: the general presumption is against using caps.

Their use should be to denote something that is unique. The Pill immediately spells the contraceptive pill and the Forces indicates that we are talking about Britain's military and not the forces of light.

Royalty: at second mention use upper case for royalty (the Prince), and also ex-royalty (the Duchess).

Ministers: always cap up posts when giving their full title, e.g. Chancellor of the Exchequer, Secretary of State for Defence. Subsequently "the Chancellor", "the Defence Secretary". With lower ranking ministers give their full title with caps (the Minister for Roads, the Minister for Higher Education) but afterwards "the minister". All foreign government jobs take lc.

Opposition posts are all lower case: xxxx the shadow chancellor. Also: the shadow cabinet; the national executive committee; the Labour Party conference. The word Opposition, when used to describe the second largest party in the House of Commons, takes the cap. However, since the Treasury always takes a cap, write shadow chief secretary to the Treasury.

For other office holders, cap up at first mention when giving full title (The Archbishop of York) but then lc (the archbishop).The National Lottery, lottery thereafter. Note Commissions, Trusts, etc are lower case after the initial full name: i.e. The Millennium Commission, the European Commission, the National Trust, thereafter become the commission, the trust. Use lower case for the names of councils, e.g. Sometown district council.

The Civil Service (but civil servants), the Services (meaning Armed Forces), but the fire service, the police service, social services (except in titles). East and West, Left and Right in politics, North, South East as names of regions, but north of Watford, west of Bristol.

Lower case for government when used adjectivally (a government spokesman, government policy); also for state, press. In England, the North, the South etc, but "he moved north". The South East, but "storms hit south-east England".

Eastern Europe, but east London: use cap when making a political rather than geographic division, thus Eastern v Western politics.

Use acronyms for well-known organisations. Some, such as Nato, can stand alone but others need explanation. When there is no acronym, avoid repetition of clusters of initials by using a variant of the title of the organisation as in: (RMT) the union, the transport workers.

capitalising words at the beginning of stories. If the first word of a news story has fewer than three letters, also cap the second. If a story begins with a name, cap fore and surnames. If this rule appears difficult to use, rewrite the intro. See also sections Names and Titles and Places and Peoples.

captions: do not tell the reader what he or she can see perfectly well in the picture ("a man stands on his head while balancing a bucket of water on the soles of his feet"). When writing the "bullet" start to captions avoid creaking puns and keep an eye on taste. A caption to a picture of a funeral might do well to drop the bullet if no better effort than "RIP: xxxxx" or "At rest: xxxxx" (both have been published elsewhere) can be found. See also tenses. Picture captions do not have full stops at the end.

In stories where we are running the pictures of several dead, avoid using the same bullet "Dead: xxxxx" half a dozen times. The repetition can seem crass and unfeeling.

carat: a measurement of weight for jewellery. Not to be confused with the vegetable.

carbon dioxide: feel free to use CO_2 — the scientific formulation — with the help of the subscript function. Do not use full-sized numeral.

carcase: carcass is American.

carnage is a loaded word and should be used precisely. It means extensive or indiscriminate slaughter. It does not mean a motorway pile-up.

car park, not parking lot.

Catholics: Roman Catholic at first mention. Many Christians in other denominations regard themselves as Catholics.

caviar, no e on the end.

CD-Rom

celebrity: use sparingly to describe somebody enjoying 15 minutes of fame. When describing somebody known for a particular talent, say what they are: singer, actor and so on.

Center Parcs

Central Saint Martins: no apostrophe.

centre on/upon, not centre around.

century: lc c for 20th century, etc.

chairman even when she is a woman. Chair, except in direct quotes, means a piece of furniture.

champagne: should only be used to denote the real thing and is not capped; for other similar products use sparkling wine.

Channel 4: use figures to denote Radio 3, Radio 4, etc, but the television channels are BBC One, BBC Two, etc. See brands.

Channel tunnel, lower case t.

charolais/charollais: one l for cattle, 2 l's for sheep.

Château d'Yquem

Chavez, Hugo

cheese: most British and French cheeses are specific to a place. Therefore, when writing their names, cap them up: red Leicester, Cornish yarg, Wensleydale, Pont l'Eveque, Camembert. As cheddar has become a generic term used worldwide, it is lower case.

Cheltenham Ladies' College: note apostrophe.

Chennai – Fomerly known as Madras, changed by the state government in 1996.

child care is a two-word term: see also health care.

ChildLine

child minder

choice: the phrase "two choices" is illogical. Where there are options, there is a single choice. Two choices would mean there are two sets of options between which two separate choices can be made.

cholesterol

Christ Church Oxford (not Christ Church College).

Christian names: refer to first names or forenames if there is doubt about the person's membership of the Christian Church or tradition. Adults should not be referred to by their first names. Minors may be.

Christie's/Christies: with apostrophe for auction houses, but Christies for the company and offshoots (e.g. Christies International plc).

Christmas lunch is what most of our readers would eat, not Christmas dinner. Use the latter only if referring specifically to an evening meal on Christmas Day.

church: capitalise for the institution, even when only one denomination is meant; lower case for buildings and plural references to denominations. (Members of many churches heard the sermon about sin. The bishop said the Church's teaching was that it was wrong.)

Cinque Ports. A group of five medieval ports in Kent and East Sussex.

church: capitalise for the institution, even when only one denomination is meant; lower case for buildings and plural references to denominations. (Members of many churches heard the sermon about sin. The bishop said the Church's teaching was that it was wrong.)

Citizens Advice Bureau: no possessive. (Plural bureaus.)

City Hall (for London).

CJD: only vCJD is the so-called human form of mad cow disease.

claim should be used only when the suggestion that someone is lying or wrong: treat with care.

Claridge's

Clarks shoes

Clause Four

clichés. Too many to list, but avoid these to start with: at the end of the day, everyone wants a piece of him, a slice of the action, to die for, kick-start, sea-change, Tinseltown, Big Apple, personal demons, day job, wake-up call, early hours, red faces, banana skins, set alarm bells ringing, assume the mantle of, caught between a rock and a hard place, anyone behaving badly, emotional roller coaster, baptism of fire, hauntingly or achingly beautiful, hits the ground running, meteoric rise, rich vein or rich seam, safe pair of hands, veritable feast, laid bare, history was made last night, hotly deny, lashed out, merry widow, red or green light, furious or bitter rows, shock report, sweet smell of success, thin on the ground, wannabe, told *The Daily Telegraph*.

Clinton: Hillary with two l's.

Clostridium difficile: first mention, *Clostridium difficile*, then *C. difficile*.

Co: as an abbreviation for company, use only in the registered names of businesses. Company names should shed Ltd or PLC except in the rare cases where it is needed to avoid confusion with personal names.

Cobbleigh, Uncle Tom.

Coca-Cola

coco pops

Cold War

colleges: many schools use college as part of their names. The word is often superfluous at first mention, and they are always "the school" after first mention.

Oxbridge colleges and halls:

OXFORD: All Souls, Balliol, Brasenose, Christ Church, Corpus Christi, Exeter, Green Templeton College, Hertford, Jesus, Keble, Kellogg, Lady Margaret Hall, Linacre, Lincoln, Magdalen, Merton, New College, Nuffield, Oriel, Pembroke, Queen's, St Anne's, St Antony's, St Catherine's, St Cross, St Edmund Hall, St John's, St Peter's, Trinity, University, Wadham, Wolfson, Worcester, Campion Hall, St Benet's Hall, Mansfield, Regent's Park, Greyfriars, St Hilda's, St Hugh's, Somerville.

CAMBRIDGE: Christ's, Churchill, Clare, Clare Hall, Corpus Christi, Darwin, Downing, Emmanuel, Fitzwilliam, Girton, Gonville and Caius (Caius at second mention), Jesus, King's, Magdalene, New Hall became Murray Edwards College in June 2008, Newnham, Pembroke, Peterhouse, Queens', Robinson, St Catharine's, St Edmund's, St John's, Selwyn, Sidney Sussex, Trinity, Trinity Hall, Wolfson. Cambridge University also includes approved societies: Homerton, Hughes Hall, Lucy Cavendish Collegiate Society.

The use of college in the names of colleges is sometimes superfluous or a solecism. Never use Christ Church College or Peterhouse College. Note spelling of Magdalen and Magdalene, Queen's and Queens', St Catherine's and St Catharine's. Always New College in full.

collisions occur between moving things or people. Cars hit trees, they do not collide with them.

colon: precedes an explanation, example or list. The colon's function is to deliver the goods invoiced in the preceding words. It links two grammatically complete clauses but makes a step forward from the intro to the main theme.

Colosseum: Rome. The London opera house is the Coliseum.

comedic: pompous Americanism, use comic. The noun is comedian.

common sense: two words as nouns, one as an adjective.

Communion, Holy

Communist should be capped only in references to people

who are members of Communist parties (he has communist views on some subjects).

compare to/compare with: with compares like with like (this year's figures compared with last year's), whereas to is descriptive or allegorical — "Shall I compare thee to a summer's day" (but compare one summer's day with another). Therefore, most usages in news will require with.

comparative prices: it is fatuous to compare prices across the ages. Remember that what sounds a niggardly sum today may have been a small — or a large — fortune at the time. This applies particularly to sale prices and wages.

comparatives are used to compare two things: the younger brother; more talented. (See superlatives for comparing more than two things).

comprise: the whole comprises the parts. "The collection comprises nuts, bolts and washers." It never takes of.

Condé Nast

confidant/confidante: note the gender difference.

Congress in the United States is made up of the Senate and the House of Representatives. We do not use Congressman John Smith; use John Smith, a member of Congress, or, more specifically, John Smith a member of the House of Representatives. Senator John Smith. Accord senators their title at first mention, but "Mr", "Mrs" or "Miss" subsequently. See names and titles section.

consecutive – not back to back.

consensus: consensus of opinion is tautological.

Conservative for members of the party and its policies, but lower case for conservative attitudes.

consonants are doubled in certain circumstances before the suffixes -able, -age, -ed, -en, -er, -ery, -ing, -ish, -y. e.g. regret/regrettable, flat/flattish, rob/robbery, clan/clannish, dim/dimmer, top/topping. Do not double h, w, x, y: washable, stowage, taxed, braying. Normally double the final consonant if it is preceded by a vowel sound denoted by a single letter in monosyllables, or if a single vowel is stressed in the final syllable of longer words: setting, rigging, repelling, formatting. In words not stressed on the final syllable, double only the letter "l" before suffixes beginning with a vowel: devilling, but appearing. Otherwise the final consonant of such stem words is not doubled.

Verbs. Most verbs ending in -fer double the "r" before -ed and -ing but not before -able: referred, conferring, but offered, offering. Silent final consonants are not doubled. There are many exceptions to these rules. Note: benefited, handicapped humbugged, kidnapped, paralleled, paralleling, picketed, woolly, woollen. Many compound words follow the rule for monosyllables (horsewhipped, leapfrogged).

consumer prices index (CPI). See retail prices index.

Continent should be capped when used as a synonym for Europe: they spent a week motoring on the Continent.

continuous describes something uninterrupted; continual allows a break. There was a continuous line of people; there were continual interruptions.

contractions: the likes of I'd, it's, can't, etc should be confined to quotes. While they may confer informality on the style of a column, they may equally grate and become irritating if overused.

convince/persuade. The former is to cause someone to be believe in the veracity of something; the latter is, through reasoned argument, to induce someone to do something. (See persuade.)

co-operate takes the hyphen.

co-operative but capped in references to the Co-operative movement. Co-op in heads.

coordinate: no hyphen.

copyright: at the end of copyrighted text, correct is: John Smith 2010.

coronation is lower case unless referring to a specific event: each new monarch has a coronation; the Coronation of King George VI was in 1937.

Correlation: two rs, one l

Côte d'Azur

Councillor is abbreviated to Cllr.

Counter Terrorism Command (So15)

country: it. Ship: she.

Country Landowners' Association

Coward, Sir Noël

crackdown — to be used sparingly.

Cradock, Fanny

crash: the word should only be used in the most extreme circumstances when describing a fall in share prices. Markets are today so volatile that its use to describe a one-day precipitate fall may be an exaggeration. To use the word legitimately there has to have been not merely a steep fall — at least 10 per cent — but also a sustained fall over two or three days. Equally, avoid other emotive terms like "plunge" or "dive", or, in the other direction, "soar" or "rocket". Also avoid the conceit that billions of pounds or dollars may be "wiped off" the price of shares. Give the facts as soberly as possible and let the readers make up their own minds.

crescendo/climax — crescendo is a rising dynamic resulting, in most cases, in a climax.

crisis: make sure it is before you use the word. Genuine crises are exceptionally rare.

Cruella de Vil

Crufts: no apostrophe (ignore *Oxford Dictionary for Writers and Editors*).

cruise missile: lc "c".

crusades, the. But cap in specific crusades: the First Crusade, etc.

curb: is the US noun for kerb, the thing that runs down the sides of roads in Britain. On both sides of the Atlantic it is also a check or restraint upon something and a verb meaning to check or restrain. See Kerb.

currency short forms of developing economic powerhouses: Brazil, the real. Short form R$; China, the renminbi, also called the yuan, its principal unit. Short form CNY; India, India rupees. Short form INR; Russia, the rouble. Short form RUB. (See Numbers, Measures and Money.)

Currys

curtsy

D

Darling, Alistair

dashes: promiscuous use of these must be avoided when a comma would suffice.

data are plural.

database: one word.

dates: Jan 1 1999, April 1 1066, AD 1066, 200 BC. Abbreviate only Jan, Feb, Aug, Sept, Oct, Nov, Dec. Use days of the week instead of dates for events within a week of the day of publication of an item. Dates such as Fourth of July, the Glorious First of June should not be made to conform to style.

The Daily Telegraph takes the article except when used adjectivally and is italicised. Same with *The Times, The Guardian,* etc. But *Daily Mail, Evening Standard.* Follow the respective mastheads. See brands.

Day-Glo

Day-Lewis, Daniel and Cecil

dead. The thorny question is when to remove the honorific from dead people. In obituaries it is immediate. We would not, though, write a news story about someone's death without calling them "Mr Smith" or "Sir John". Once the funeral has taken place, Smith should suffice at second and subsequent mentions. Royalty retain their titles after death: King George, Queen Elizabeth, Diana, Princess of Wales. Murder victims retain honorifics until after the trial.

Debrett's

decades: write out Thirties, Fifties, etc. It reads better than 1930s.

decimal points should appear at the bottom of a character, not halfway up it: thus 9.5.

decimate means to reduce by a tenth. Use only literally.

de facto and de jure are such accepted terms in the English language that they do not need to be italicised.

defense secretary: this what the US has.

defrocked/unfrocked: prefer unfrocked.

defuse/diffuse. The former is to make a bomb harmless by removing its fuse, or to make a situation less tense or dangerous. Diffuse, the verb, to scatter in many directions; the adjective describes something that is widely spread.

degree signs (raised zeros) are omitted in temperatures. The abbreviations F and C indicate degrees.

de Klerk, de Gaulle, but De Niro and DeVito.

de Mille, Cecil B

Delves Broughton

Deng Xiaoping

Dennis the Menace

deny: to deny something, one has to be accused of something first. Despite the ancient usage, it does not now mean to offer a contrary view.

Department for Environment, Food and Rural Affairs, Department of Health, and so on, all become lower case departments in later references.

dependants are people, often children, who depend on others. They are dependent.

deserts: "just deserts" is right. It comes from the verb to deserve.

dessert: final course of a meal.

Desert Rats: only the 7th Armoured Brigade with service in North Africa 1941–42, Iraq 1991 and 2003. Never in heads, sparing use in copy.

despoil: noun is despoliation or despoilment, but not despoilation.

Deutsche Grammophon

devastated: use if a large geographical area has been obliterated by forces of war or nature, never to describe someone who has suffered grief or disappointment.

Diana, Princess of Wales, subsequently the Princess, never Diana except in headlines.

Di Caprio, Leonardo.

dietitian

different from.

diphthongs: two vowel sounds pronounced as one syllable as in the word "out" or "mound". Follow the *Concise Oxford Dictionary* unless there is a specific style ruling.

director-general of the BBC is not capped.

disc/disk: computer disks — otherwise, discs.

disclose is always better than reveal. But still avoid if possible.

discreet/discrete: the former means tactful or prudent; the latter separate.

disfranchised, not disenfranchised.

disinterested means lacking motive for showing bias or favouritism. A referee should not be uninterested in a football match, but he should remain disinterested by not having a bet on the result.

Disney: it is Disneyland, California; Disney World, Florida; Disneyland Paris, France.

Dispatch Box in the Commons.

dissociate: not disassociate.

divorce: when referring to a previous marriage say "his first marriage ended in divorce" or "was dissolved", but do not go into details, except in special circumstances. Take care to ensure all facts are correct and verified.

Doctor (abbreviate to Dr) should generally be used only as a title in references to people with medical qualifications. However, members of other professions in which a different sort of doctorate is a relevant qualification should be accorded that title – notably university dons or members of scientific research institutes. Indicate the nature of other doctorates when the title is used for people other than physicians. Surgeons prefer to be called Mr, but always indicate their qualifications or specialty.

dogs: the breed names are lower case – fox terrier, poodle – except when a geographical term or adjective derived from a nationality or British location precedes the term for a type of dog – Irish wolfhound, West Highland terrier, Old English sheepdog, Border collies and Alsatians.

dog-whistle politics is jargon. If used within quotation marks supply glossary for the reader; otherwise avoid.

Dolce & Gabbana

Dolittle, Dr

Domesday Book: thus

Doolittle, Eliza

Dorchester, The – is its name.

Dostoevsky

dotcom

double entendre is bad French: they would say *double entente*.

doyen/doyenne: the most respected man or woman in a particular sphere of activity.

Dr Martens

draconian: Draco was a maker of harsh laws. Use this adjective only in a legal or regulatory context; otherwise use harsh or severe.

drama: in a non-theatrical context, tabloid. Use exceptionally sparingly.

dreamt, not dreamed.

drink-drive limits: Breath: 35 micrograms per 100 millilitres of breath; Blood: 80 milligrams per 100 millilitres of blood; Urine: 107 milligrams per 100 millilitres of urine. If a breath test is positive, but under 50 micrograms per 100 millilitres, then a blood or urine test is needed before a prosecution can be brought; above 50, a breath test alone is strong enough to be used as evidence.

dubbed, is derived from the provision of a voice soundtrack for film or television. Not to be used in the context of assigning a name or title to somebody or something. Commentators dubbed *The Daily Telegraph* an Establishment newspaper.

Duchess of Cornwall is never Camilla. In headlines, "Duchess" on its own is acceptable.

Duchess of York is never Fergie. And no longer HRH.

due to is used adjectivally and, therefore, needs a noun to modify (his lateness was due to rain, not he was late due to rain). Illogically, there is no similar rule for "owing to". The use of "because" solves problems in this area (He was late because of rain) and is preferred.

duffel coat

Duke of Edinburgh is preferred to Prince Philip, with "the Duke" subsequently. Duke of York is preferred to Prince Andrew, with "the Duke" subsequently.

E

e, when to omit: the silent e at the end of a word is dropped, in most cases, before suffixes beginning with a vowel, and, in most cases, retained before suffixes beginning with a consonant. The many exceptions include:

Words ending in -ce and ge retain the e to indicate the softness of the consonant (peaceable, changeable) but, illogically, the e is dropped after soft g before the suffixing in words like changing, raging (but ageing). ee, oe and ye remain intact (canoeing, dyeing, eyeing, fleeing).

The e is retained before -able in adjectives formed from verbs ending in -le after a consonant (handle becomes handleable).

Some of the problem words are: blameable, hireable, likeable, rateable, shakeable, routeing (to distinguish taking a direction from routing or putting to flight) singeing, swingeing (to distinguish from singing, swinging), linage (source of additional income for provincial journalists), lineage (ancestry), judgment.

-ed, -n or -t in past tense and past participles: burnt, dreamt, knelt, leant, leapt, learnt, smelt, spelt, spilt, spoilt (but despoiled). Most others use -ed, but note bereft (of property), bereaved (by death), cloven hoof, cleft palate, cleft stick, cleaved (used axe). Earned (not earnt). Hewn, mown, sawn (sawnoff shotgun), shorn (not sheared of one's hair), shown, sown, strewn, swollen for past participles, but past tense hewed, mowed, sawed, sheared, showed, sowed, strewed, swelled.

-er or **-or**: there is no rule except to follow the Oxford dictionaries. The living suffix -er is used in most newly minted words, but -or is often added to Latin words for technical terms. Normally -ator, but debater. Note: protester, demonstrator, adapter (one who adapts), adaptor (electrical), castor (sprinkler), censer (incense vessel), censor (the journalist's enemy), conveyer (person), conveyor (machine), resister (person), resistor (electrical). Legal terms often depart from normal forms.

each is singular.

Earls Court: the exhibition hall has no possessive, but the Tube station and neighbourhood is Earl's Court.

early hours is hackneyed. Early on its own is often enough.

earth takes a capital only when used as the proper name of the planet; in this sense, it does not need the definite article.

east: capitalise in references to regions or international politics. Lower case for points of the compass. See Places and Peoples.

EastEnders

Easter Saturday falls the Saturday after Easter Sunday. The day between Good Friday and Easter Sunday is Holy Saturday.

easyJet

E. coli takes italics. No need to spell it out in full at first mention.

ecstasy but give the drug the cap E.

editions/issues: be accurate with our own trade jargon.

educationist, not educationalist.

Edwardian: Edward VII reigned from 1901 to 1910.

effect as a verb means to cause; as a noun it means result. Affect as a verb means to influence or to assume a guise or pretence. As a noun it has a limited role as a term in psychology.

e.g. for example. Takes points.

eisteddfod, eisteddfodau (pl).

either/neither, the first a noun, which describes a choice between alternatives – an either/or situation. The second, a determiner or pronoun, which articulates not one or the other of two people or things. Neither option is desirable if used incorrectly. Verbs should agree with the nearer subject (either the soldiers or Mary is wrong). (See N.)

eke out means to make something last longer.

elder of two, eldest of three or more.

electrocute: means death from electric shock. There are no survivors.

email

embarrass: double r, double s. Note harass, one r.

embassy: the British Embassy, the Russian Embassy, but the embassy is lower case.

emerge: only from the deep, or the darkness. Phrases like "it emerged yesterday" to describe something that has come to light are hackneyed and tired.

Emin, Tracey

Encyclopaedia Britannica, otherwise encyclopedia.

engineers are professionally qualified people. Do not use for even the most skilled manual workers; they are engineering workers.

enormity is a moral term, describing a condition of wickedness or outrageousness. It does not mean large.

enquire, enquiry: do not use. Inquire and inquiry are preferred.

ensure (make certain), insure (reduce monetary risk).

epitome of is a cliché and is to be avoided.

Equator

Eriksson, Sven-Goran

erupt is what volcanoes and pustules do. Rows, arguments and other disputes break out.

escaper or escaped man. Not escapee.

etc should not have a full point if used, but it should be avoided where possible. In full two words, et cetera.

euro: the currency, plural euros.

European Convention on Human Rights

European Court of Human Rights

European Parliament: Euro-MP, member of the European Parliament. MEP is also acceptable.

Europhobe: this word is banned.

Europol: this is a European agency and should not be described as "a European police force".

Eurosceptic: Cap E, one word.

Eurostar is an international passenger train service between Britain and France and Belgium. It is not to be confused with Eurotunnel, which owns the tunnel through which it passes.

ex as in ex-president Smith is hyphenated and not capped. Former is often better.

exam is to be used only in heads: examination is to be used in text.

Exchequer takes a capital.

exclamation marks: except in some quotes, these have no place in *The Daily Telegraph*.

exclusive: use it properly, to mean shutting out or

preventing entry or participation. It is never to be used as a synonym for "rich" or "expensive".

executions are carried out in accordance with military or judicial orders; terrorists and gangsters kill, murder or assassinate people.

existing arrangements verges on the tautological.

expel: one l, but expelled.

expert: be careful how you use this word. It tends to be applied to almost anyone who claims a passing knowledge of the subject.

explorer Scouts

extra as a prefix meaning outside does not take a hyphen, except before a capital letter or the letter a (extraordinary, extramural, extra-European). Use the hyphen when extra used adjectivally means that something is unusual because of size or degree (extra-long extra-dry).

eyewitness: prefer witness in nearly all cases, although sometimes the precision is needed.

F

fact that: the phrase "the fact that" often just means "because". Avoid.

Fairtrade

Faithfull, Marianne

famous: if someone really is you don't need the adjective.

Fanu: Dr James Le Fanu

Farhi, Nicole

Faroes

farther: for distances; further means additional.

fascist and fascism are capitalised only in references to groups who call or called themselves Fascists. As general descriptions, usually abusive, they take lower case (he said the policeman was a fascist). Most modern groups are lower-case neo-fascists.

Father is used at second mention in references to priests of the Roman Catholic and some other churches. Some Anglican priests also prefer this title, and it may be used if there is no danger of confusion. Abbreviate to Fr only in lists or when the meaning is obvious.

Father Christmas is preferred to Santa.

Fayed rule: no name affectations such as al or van. If someone holds such a name by birth, for example von

Hapsburg, or al-Khalifa, rather than having styled himself with it, then use it.

Federico Fellini, the Italian film director.

fed up: we should soon become fed up with the ignorant usage "fed up of".

feel-good factor is a cliché and should be avoided.

Femmes fatales: note in French both noun and adjective are pluralised.

feng shui

fettuccine

fewer is used for numbers of people or things; less applies to quantities. Use less, even with figures, when a sum or quantity is suggested (fewer than 100 people attended, ate less than a ton of steak, and paid less than £100).

fiancé, man; fiancée, woman. Note the acute accent.

fill in forms: we fill out our clothes after over-eating.

filmic is an American adjective that has no place in the English language so long as cinematic exists.

film titles: if in doubt, consult IMDb.co.uk, which is the definitive source of reference for these (see Bridge on the River Kwai).

Finnegans Wake has no apostrophe, except as the name of the ballad, which the book is named after.

Finnigan, Judy

firefighter: use fireman (firewoman) instead. There is an RAF rank of fireman. Firefighters only if you know there was a woman in the team.

firing line: note that to be in the firing line means to be in the line-up of people shooting at someone else (i.e. an execution squad). To be "in the line of fire" is to be fired at.

firm, as a noun, usually means partnership and should not be used as a synonym for company. Legal issues may be involved.

First Lady takes caps.

First World War, not World War One. Also Great War.

flammable not inflammable. The negative is non-flammable. Speeches remain inflammatory.

flaunt/flout: flaunt = display ostentatiously; flout = treat with contempt.

flier, not flyer.

focused/focusing: one s not two.

foetus: not fetus.

Fogg: Phileas, not Phineas.

following should not be used to mean coming after in time. Use after.

for, fore as prefixes: for implies prohibition or abstention.

Fore is used in words needing the sense of being before or in advance of something (forecourt, foreshadow). Forego means to go before, forgo means to give up or go without. Forbear/forebear: forbear = desist; forebear = an ancestor. Foresee: not forsee.

Foreign and Commonwealth Office at first mention. FCO subsequently.

foreign words: these should almost never be used in news, except in direct quotes or as part of proper names (e.g. Quai d'Orsay). Do not italicise such proper names but do italicise other foreign words. There is more licence to use foreign terms in feature writing, but only sparingly, and only when the terms used are familiar to our educated readership through their frequent use in English. Also note that where American and Australian spellings differ in official titles, such as defense secretary and Labor Party, we use their spellings.

forensic means of or used in courts of law, and it is misleading to use "forensic experts" to describe scientists and technicians who help to investigate crime. They are forensic scientists, pathologists, experts, etc. The *Oxford Dictionary of English* also describes it as "the application of scientific methods and techniques to the investigation of crime". Care must be taken to use this definition in its correct context.

formulas, not formulae.

Forsyth, Freddie and Bruce.

THE TELEGRAPH STYLE GUIDE

founder/flounder, both verbs, the first is to fill a ship with water and sink it or the failure of an undertaking because of a particular problem. The talks between Labour and the Liberal Democrats foundered on the issue of the single European currency. To flounder is to struggle, more often than not in water. It is also to struggle mentally, or show great confusion.

foxhunting is one word.

Francis of Assisi: St Francis was a friar, not a priest.

freedom of cities, etc. Beware being given the Freedom of the City and being made an honorary freeman/freewoman are different. Make sure which one we are talking about.

Freud, Lucian

fuel, fine when talking about energy but hackneyed when used instead of provoke.

fulfils: be sparing with the l's.

fuller is a nonsense: if something is full it cannot get any fuller. Avoid (see incomparable adjectives).

fullness: preferred to fulness.

full stops: no full stops after initials in a name. (J D Smith.) See different rule for bylines under initials.

fulsome means cloying or excessive not copious, and is often pejorative.

fund, as a verb, is often a bureaucratic way of saying pay for, but it has a precise meaning as a financial term.

fury: be very selective in its use.

G

Gaddafi

Gandhi

gale: the wind must reach 39 mph to qualify. Avoid gale-force winds. Strong gales begin at 47 mph, storms at 64 mph and hurricanes at 73 mph. See Beaufort scale.

Garden of Eden

Gardner, Ava

Garry Kasparov: the world chess champion now uses two r's. Not Gary, nor Gari.

GATT: General Agreement on Tariffs and Trade. Always explain. Now superseded by the World Trade Organisation.

Gauloises

Le Gavroche: not La.

gay: permissible in headlines if essential but use homosexual in text.

gelatin: no final e.

gender is a grammatical classification; sex is the biology.

general election: lower case.

Gentleman's Relish

genuine: do not overuse this already rather exhausted word.

Georgian: George I came to the throne in 1714, George IV died in 1830.

German nouns: if used as foreign words, and therefore italicised, they must take an initial cap: e.g *Weltanschauung.* Otherwise, if used as word that has passed into English, neither italicise nor cap up, e.g. schadenfreude. Umlauts in German words should remain at all times and not have an 'e' inserted to lengthen the vowel.

Gielgud, Sir John

ginger group is political jargon. Avoid. See also policy wonk and dog-whistle politics.

gipsy: not gypsy.

girlfriend is not a synonym for mistress.

girls become women at the age of 18.

Giuliani, Rudy

glasnost – do not italicise.

GNP: gross national product at first mention, then GNP, but always explain.

gobbledegook

God takes a capital in all references to the Supreme Being of monotheist religions – Christ, Jesus, Holy Spirit, Holy Ghost and Allah. Capitalise He, Him, His, Thee, Thou but not who, whom. References to pagan gods are lower case but capitalise individual gods (Thor, Jupiter) and individual gods of polytheist religions (Vishnu).

Goldsmiths College: no apostrophe.

goodness or goodness' sake are both correct.

Gore-Tex

goth: no caps for teenage dress code.

Government: When referring to the current British Government, all past governments of the UK and all foreign governments are lower case. The British Government is Her Majesty's Government. It does not belong to the Prime Minister, so it is not to be referred to as "David Cameron's government". It is "David Cameron's administration".

governors-general in plural.

Graceland

Grade I or Grade II listed: no hyphens.

graffiti

grams, not grammes.

grapes: see wines.

Great Britain: see United Kingdom.

Greene, Graham

greenhouse gases, greenhouse effect.

Green Paper

Grossman, Loyd

Guantánamo has an accent.

guerrilla

guillotine motion: explain that it limits debate.

Guildhall (in London) not the Guildhall.

the Gulf: not Iranian, Persian or Arabian.

Guns N' Roses (only one apostrophe).

gunwale, no h.

Guy's and St Thomas' hospital trust and hospitals.

gybe for the nautical activity. Jibe for sneer.

H

habeas corpus

Habsburg not Hapsburg.

hackneyed phrases, in an organisation such as the Telegraph Media Group these are not to die for and must be avoided in industrial quantities.

Hague, Ffion

hairdryer, not drier.

Hallowe'en: with the apostrophe.

Hallyday, Johnny: chanteur.

Hamleys: no apostrophe.

Hammarskjold, Dag

Hamnett, Katharine

handout is not a synonym for benefit. It is also tabloid. Use with extreme care.

handover: no hyphen.

hanged/hung: people, at least unlucky ones, are hanged; pictures, pheasants and our Parliament are hung.

Hannah, Daryl

harass, but embarrass.

hardliner: be very selective in its use.

hard-pressed is becoming clichéd and ubiquitous. Use only if all else fails.

hare-brained, not hair.

Harley-Davidson

Harman, Harriet: Miss. Her married name is Mrs Dromey.

HarperCollins: one word.

Harper's Bazaar

Harpers & Queen

Harrods: no apostrophe.

Harvey Nichols

hawks and doves: this is becoming a cliché, so use sparingly in descriptions of the relative levels of aggression or conciliation between two factions — do not use when referring to the IRA or other terrorist groups to try to distinguish between different degrees of ruthlessness.

H-bomb: but nuclear weapon is often the better term.

headmaster, headmistress: lower case; some schools (such as St Paul's) have high masters. Eton has a Head Master. Radley has a Warden and Wellington a Master. Never call the headmaster of a boys' public school the head teacher: this term should only be used about mixed-sex schools that might be as likely to appoint a headmistress as a headmaster.

head of state, head of government. A distinction must be drawn between the two. The Queen is our head of

State, David Cameron our head of Government. Across the Channel, in the Republic of France, Mr Sarkozy is both.

health care, not healthcare.

heartbreak: tabloid, avoid.

heart failure, heart condition: every heart has some condition and heart failure is often a sign of death, not its cause.

heart-rending, not heart-wrenching.

Heathcliff

heave: verb, to lift or haul something heavy with great effort. The past participle is heaved or hove.

Hello! magazine

Hells Angels: no apostrophe.

Helmand

hero: should not be used except in cases where it is demonstrably correct, as with winners of the VC or GC. Its use in lesser contexts debases it.

hiccup: not hiccough.

Hi-De-Hi!

High Church

High Commissions, High Commissioners: the equivalent of embassies and ambassadors within the Commonwealth.

They are capitalised according to the same rules.

high street as an adjective is often redundant: shops, banks and other emporia to which it is applied are rarely found in the middle of fields.

hijack: the seizure of any vehicle — land, sea or air — without lawful reason. The original meaning of criminals stealing from criminals is too restrictive. Skyjacking may still be used.

hike: a long walk, not a rise in prices.

Hindi (language), Hindu (religion), Hindustani was a pidgin Hindi used by British soldiers in India.

Hinkley Point: no "c".

Hippocratic oath: the oath doctors take; after Hippocrates (ca 460 BC to ca 370 BC), the Greek physician.

history: phrases such as "history was made last night" are to be avoided, because in one sense history is being made every night, and in others it is hardly ever being made at all.

hi-tech: not high-tech

Hizbollah: not Hezbollah.

hoard is a store of food or treasure: horde is a multitude.

Hobson's Choice is not the lesser of two evils. It is not a choice at all.

hoi polloi: the people. Hoi is the definite article, so don't say "the".

hold-up for delays or crimes, but hold up as verb.

Holiday, Billie

Holocaust: cap up when used to describe the Nazi genocide. Lower case in other uses, but ensure you use it legitimately to describe mass destruction.

Holy Communion takes caps.

home nations does not take caps.

home owner, not homeowner. Use cautiously in the context of mortgages.

homoeopathy, thus. Royal London Homoeopathic Hospital, but Homeopathic Trust and Faculty of Homeopathy.

homogeneous: having the same constituent elements throughout, used for people, communities, etc that have homogeneity. Do not confuse with: homogenous, which is a form of milk.

homophobic: an extreme and irrational aversion to homosexuals and homosexuality. Use sparingly, but sometimes it is unavoidable as it is often used, for example, by police when describing an assault.

homophones and homonyms: A homophone is a word that sounds the same as another but has a different spelling and meaning, e.g. insight/incite. A homonym is a word with the same spelling and sound but a different meaning, e.g. kind (helpful), kind (type).

homosexual is an adjective, not a noun.

Hooray Henrys

hopefully: another ignorant Americanism. Do not misuse for "it is hoped that". Its correct use in English is as an adverb: "to travel hopefully".

horrify: use only literally, and therefore sparingly.

Horse Guards Parade

horse riding: just say "riding".

horsy

hosepipe

hospitalised is a vile Americanism: use "taken (or admitted) to hospital".

hospital trust names: at first use cap up as follows – St George's Healthcare NHS Trust, then subsequently the trust. St Bartholomew's Hospital and The Royal London Hospital are both run by Barts and The London NHS Trust: the The must be capped.

hosting: see staging.

hotspot: one word

Howards End

Howerd, Frankie

HRH/HM as the abbreviations for His/Her Royal Highness and His/Her Majesty are styles, not titles. Of living British royalty, only the Queen is HM.

huge things rarely are, is banned.

humble: do not use it in coy phrases such as "the humble sixpence". If an object is so mundane or prosaic as to call the concept to mind, the adjective is redundant. It is perfectly all right when properly describing a person's demeanour.

hummus

Humphrys, John

huntsman: each hunt has one, usually a paid hunt servant. Other people who hunt with the aid of hounds (never dogs) are members of the hunt or the field. Shooting is not classed as hunting. Use wildfowling, rough shooting, game shooting, stalking, etc as appropriate.

Hyannisport

hyperthermia: condition of having body-temperature much above normal.

hypothermia: condition of having body-temperature much below normal.

hyphens. Compound words increasingly lose their hyphens as they are accepted as normal usage, and reference to a newly edited *Oxford English Dictionary* is often necessary. With most prefixes and suffixes the compound is written as a single word, but ex-, neo-, non-, pro- and self- usually need hyphens, but note selfsame and unselfconscious. Co- meaning fellow, as in co-driver, takes the hyphen.

Hyphens are also used to mark the difference between

similar words (reform, re-form), to separate identical vowels (pre-empt, co-operate, but uncooperative), before stems beginning with a capital letter (pro-British) and with -like when it follows words ending in -l (eel-like) or words of more than one syllable (reporter-like). The suffix -less needs the hyphen after stems ending with -ll (hill-less).

Hyphens are normally used in compound adjectives formed from a noun and a participle (cloud-filled sky) or from an adverb and a verb (well-written prose). But do not use the hyphen after adverbs ending in -ly (newly married couple), and note that adverbs and verbs used after nouns remain separate (a well-oiled machine, but the machine was well oiled). Note that a man earns £17,000 a year and so has a £17,000-a-year job. Hyphens are to be avoided in sporting terms: wicketkeeper, scrum half, etc.

Use hyphens with care to avoid confusion or unwanted hilarity.

Avoid dangling hyphens (his two- and four-year-old children).

Fractions are not hyphenated: e.g. two thirds of all acrobats, three quarters, etc; except when adjectival, as in a two-thirds majority.

No hyphens in Latin: in vitro fertilisation, post mortem examination (*Oxford Dictionary for Writers and Editors* is inconsistent on this, so ignore).

I

I and me, if in doubt about which pronoun to use, remove the rest of the phrase and see whether it makes sense. E.g. My friend and I went to the cinema. Not my friend and me went to the cinema.

ICBM: intercontinental ballistic missile. Always be precise in describing the nature of particular missiles. Long-range and similar terms are not enough.

ice cream (no hyphen).

Ideal Home show: not Homes.

ideologue

i.e.: use, with points, only when it cannot be avoided. It means "that is" and often introduces a long description of something that should have been explained properly in the first place.

if and whether: use the latter if clause makes sense with "or not" on the end of it. So one would write "he will celebrate if he passes his exams" but "he doesn't know whether he will pass his exams", not "if he will pass".

ilk: only in Scottish titles.

Immaculate Conception requires caps, and must only be used in the accurate context: to describe the belief that the Virgin Mary was from her conception without taint of sin.

impact: effect is nearly always better. Use impact in a physical sense. Impact is a noun and not a verb. Avoid constructions such as "it impacted upon" and say instead "it made an impact upon".

imply/infer: he implied that I was lazy; I inferred that he thought that I was lazy.

impostor

impractical is a relatively modern usage. It is better to say unpractical, or impracticable.

impresario

imprisoned: say jailed.

inamorata is a woman: a male lover is an inamorato.

incomparable adjectives: think of the logic before making a comparative or superlative of any adjective. Such words describing absolute conditions as empty, dead, lost and absolute cannot logically compare.

indexes not indices (except in mathematics or science).

Indian place names: Mumbai, Chennai (formerly Madras), Bangalore, Calcutta and New Delhi. (See Places and Peoples).

industrial action: prefer strike, overtime ban, work-to-rule. If such precision is impossible, use disruptive action or protest action.

inevitable should not be used when you mean customary: avoid such usages as "Mr Smith smoked his inevitable cigar".

infamous: avoid.

infinitives: basic form of a verb not bound to a particular subject or tense (See split infinitives).

ingrained, not engrained.

initials: full points to be used in by-lines where the writer uses initials rather than a first name (J. D. Smith).

inquire/enquire: our style is inquire, inquiry.

insofar as.

instill

institute/institution: always check which word is used in the title of an organisation with which you are not familiar.

interaction of, not between.

Inter Governmental Conference: caps no hyphens.

internet (lc "i").

Intifada. First Intifada, Second Intifada.

into: "in" is not an acceptable substitute (he fell into the river and swam in it). Never use "into" for an enthusiasm as in "he is into rock music".

Inuit, not Eskimos (See Places and Peoples).

invite, verb. Invitation, noun.

-ise,-isation not-ize, -ization.

iPod, iPhone, iPad: thus, see trade names.

IRA: do not, outside quotes, use the term "active service unit" for a group of terrorists from this organisation or any other with a similar *modus operandi.*

Iran is not an Arab nation.

Islamophobia

italics: use sparingly. Italicise titles of films, books, magazines, television shows, plays and paintings, and foreign words that are not current in English where sense demands they are used. Poems should be in quotation marks but collections of poems, being books, should be italicised. Songs should be italicised; the names of symphonies should be in Roman except where the symphony has a subsidiary title: for example, Beethoven's Fifth Symphony, but Vaughan Williams's Second Symphony (the London). The titles of all publications, including *The Daily Telegraph, The Sunday Telegraph* and titles of reports should be italicised. Websites should not be italicised but their status as websites made clear by the use of their domain name: Telegraph.co.uk, Google.com.

its/it's, do we really need to explain the difference?

J

Jackson-Stops & Staff: thus.

Jack Daniel's: thus.

Jacuzzi (cap J).

jail not gaol.

Jameson: Irish whiskey.

Janáček, Leoš: note accents.

Jap: do not use even in headlines.

jargon: the word is often misused as a reproachful description of terms that are properly used by experts to achieve precision and brevity. When such terms are adopted into newspaper copy, in, for instance, a report on a space flight, they must be explained at first mention. They do not need quotation marks. Do not confuse jargon with slang, but remember that jargon also means gibberish.

Jeep is a trade name for a kind of civilian vehicle and must be capped, but jeep (lc) is correct in references to small vehicles used in the Second World War. (See Trade names.)

jejune

Jenkins's ear

Jesus: it is wrong to think that Christ should always be used. In references, capitalise He, Him and His.

Jew use only as a noun. Never use Jewess.

jewellery not jewelry.

Jewish holy days: Pesach (Passover), Shavuot (Pentecost), Rosh Hashanah (New Year), Yom Kippur (Day of Atonement), Sukkot (Feast of Tabernacles). Shemini Atzeret and Simchat Torah are the eight and ninth day of Sukkot.

jibe (not gibe) for sneer. Gybe for the nautical activity.

job descriptions: be accurate when describing what somebody does for a living. Various people who are professionally untrained sing arias from operas to a mass audience. They are not opera singers. They are popular entertainers. Our readers know the difference.

job titles: David Cameron, the Prime Minister, not Prime Minister David Cameron. The titles of professional posts require the definite article: so it is "John Smith, the chairman of Smith plc", not "John Smith, chairman of Smith plc".

Johns Hopkins University, Baltimore: not John Hopkins.

Johnson, Boris: Do not refer to him as 'Boris' in text but 'Mr Johnson' or 'the Mayor'. Boris may be used in headlines if absolutely necessary.

Jonsson, Ulrika

joyrider: not an ideal term for a person who steals a car in order to get a thrill from driving it about, but the best anyone has come up with and instantly recognisable to the reader. Avoid if possible.

judgment (no "e" between the syllables).

Juneau is the state capital of Alaska. Anchorage is the largest settlement.

junk bonds: no hyphen (as City style).

the Jurassic coast is in Dorset and east Devon.

just should only be used where it describes a state of righteousness. Otherwise use merely, only or simply.

just deserts.

Justices of the Supreme Court: members of the House of Lords qualified to perform the Supreme Court's legal work. A Lord Justice of Appeal, usually a knight, does not sit in the House of Lords.

K

Kalashnikov

karaoke

Karzai, Hamid

Kasparov, Garry

Kaye, Gorden (*'Allo 'Allo!* star)

Kelley, Kitty

Kellogg's

Kent: east of Medway, man of Kent; west of Medway: Kentish man.

kerb: British version of curb, the thing that runs down the sides of US streets. See also curb.

key as a substitute for important or significant is overused.

keynote speech: usually isn't. Avoid.

Kibaki, Mwai: Kenyan politician.

Kim Il-sung

Kim Jong-il

Kim Jong-un, the third and youngest son of Kim Jong-il, and his possible successor as supreme leader of the Democratic People's Republic of Korea, North Korea.

Kinski, Nastassja

KitKat

Klebb, Rosa

Kosovo, not Kosova; Kosovans, not Kosovars.

knot is a measurement of speed. Never use knots per hour.

Ku Klux Klan

Kwik-Fit

Kwik Save

L

Labour for the party, but labour movement, organised labour: however New Labour, old Labour.

Ladies' Day at Royal Ascot.

lady: use "woman" for most references to a female. But see Names and Titles for use of Lady.

Lafite, claret.

landmark: do not use in the sense of a decision that marks an important change or precedent. All right for a prominent object on the horizon.

Land Rover

lang, k d (thus).

Langtry, Lillie

last: the last issue of *The Daily Telegraph* implies we have closed. Use "most recent" or "latest". Also prefer "the past two years" to "the last two years".

last night: tabloid, overused in news stories and to be avoided. Use only where absolutely literal: for example, "Big Ben struck thirteen at midnight last night because of a mechanical error" is fine. "It was disclosed last night that the Government is planning to slay the first born" is not, since the event probably happened during office hours. When something actually does happen just before edition time, it may be acceptable in the interests of conveying urgency.

Last Post (not the Last Post).

late: phrases like "the late John Smith" are to be avoided. The context usually makes it plain that he is dead; if it does not, say when he died. Never "widow of the late John Smith". An exception is where a living person may be confused with the deceased, hence "the late Queen Elizabeth".

Latin tags: use sparingly, where there is no better English equivalent and where there is a reasonable chance the reader will know the sense: thus de jure and de facto are acceptable, *de minimis non curat lex* probably not. Always italicise those phrases not in common usage.

latter is the second of two. For the final of more than two, last.

Laurence, Vice-Adml Tim, is the husband of the Princess Royal

lavatory is the correct term, never toilet.

lay, lie: "lay", meaning to deposit, arrange, beat down, and its past tense "laid" are transitive verbs needing an object (we decided to lay a floor; the hen laid an egg). Lie, meaning to recline or remain, and its derivatives lay and lain are intransitive (lie in the bed, the ship lay at anchor, the grass where she had lain was flattened). To use lie transitively to mean lay (lie her on the bed) is incorrect. To use lay intransitively to mean lie (it was laying on the floor) is also wrong.

leakage is the amount lost by a leak. Do not put quotation marks round the word leak in references to news released unofficially.

learnt is what one did with a lesson: learned describes an erudite person.

lease of life: if you must use this cliché please use the correct English form and not the American "lease on life".

le Carré, John

Left, Right in politics. Left wing, Left-wingers. Such terminology is however becoming increasingly meaningless, so use sparingly and with explanation.

left field: done to death.

legendary: unless you really are writing about King Arthur, avoid.

Legge-Bourke, Tiggy

legionnaires' disease: as in *Black's Medical Dictionary*.

Leibovitz, Annie

Le Manoir aux Quat'Saisons

Leonardo, never "da Vinci".

less is not the comparative of few or small. Use fewer or smaller. (See entry for fewer).

letters page style: all letters to the Editor should start Sir. Counties should not be abbreviated in addresses. Months should not be abbreviated in reference to previous correspondents. Titles should not be abbreviated.

liaise

Liberal takes a capital letter only for political parties using the name and their members. Use lower case when explaining the attitudes of foreign parties of the relative position of people within them (the liberal Free Democrats . . . A liberal Democrat won his party's nomination). But there is a small Liberal Party in the United States.

Liberal Democrats: use Lib Dems in heads, use in full on first mention in text, Lib Dems as a subsequent use is acceptable. Do not confuse with the Liberal Party, which still exists as a small and separate entity.

Libération, French newspaper: note accent.

licence: noun.

license: verb.

lifeboat, but Royal National Life-boat Institution.

lifestyle: avoid. Use "way of life".

light sabre. Although it originated in a galaxy far, far away the English rendering is preferred.

like is used only to introduce a noun not followed by a verb (he drinks like a fish. He swims as a fish swims). When giving named examples of people or objects we should use "such as" as in: he said that he admired players such as Jones, Smith and Brown. The sense is that he admires those players specifically. If we used "like" it would mean that he admired players with qualities similar to those of Jones, Smith and Brown.

likeable

likes of has a pejorative connotation, as in "My daughter's too good for the likes of you". Use "people like" or "people such as" as the meaning dictates.

Lili Marlene

limousine, limo are tabloid: write "car".

linage for number of lines; lineage for ancestry.

linchpin: person or thing essential to a plan or organisation. Not lynchpin.

literally is nearly always redundant or ridiculous (Botham literally carried the rest of the England team).

Lloyds Banking Group

Lloyd's (insurance). Lloyd's Register. Lloyd's is not an insurance company. It does not write insurance itself but provides a market in which its members do so.

Lloyd Webber. The family name is unhyphenated, the peerage — Lloyd-Webber — is.

loan is a noun, not a verb.

loathe (hate) but loath (disinclined, unwilling).

London postal districts are not preceded by a comma, hence "London SW1".

longitude: east/west of the Greenwich meridian . . . the angular distance of a place from SE10. Latitude, the angular distance of a place north or south of Earth's equator.

Lords Lieutenant: not Lord Lieutenants. Certain reference books have this wrong, so beware.

Lords Justices

Lord's (cricket).

lorry: prefer it to "truck". But if a motor company refers officially to a "trucks division", we should conform.

lounges are found in hotels and pubs. In houses they are sitting rooms or drawing rooms.

Lubyanka

lunch not luncheon except in formal social contexts.

Lurex

Lutine bell

luxury: as an adjective it is becoming tabloid, as in luxury flats. Avoid.

Lycra

Lyon, the French city in Rhône-Alpes does not have an s. (See also Marseille).

Lyttelton Theatre

M

Maasai, not Masai.

Maastricht treaty, thus.

mad cow disease: all lc. (See legionnaires' disease.)

Madama Butterfly is what Puccini wrote.

Madison Square Garden, singular.

Madras, the Indians now call it Chennai (See Mumbai and Bombay).

madrasah

Magdalen College Oxford: Magdalene College Cambridge.

Magna Carta was sealed, not signed.

maharaja

maître d', maîtres d': note accent.

major: usually means no more than "big".

majority/minority take a plural verb. See number.

Malkovich, John

Maltesers

Man Booker Prize for Fiction, the.

manoeuvre, manoeuvred, manoeuvring.

mansion: tabloid. Its use by us can only be satirical.

mantel (shelf), mantelpiece. Mantle is a cape.

Marks & Spencer

marry: do not use wed.

Marseille: a Mediterranean port in France, requires no s on its end.

marshal always has one l, whether a verb, noun or a title.

Martini & Rossi is a trade name. References specifically to their vermouth should be capped, the cocktail, which they did not invent, is simply a martini (three parts gin or vodka to one part dry vermouth, olive and a twist of lemon).

Martinů, Bohuslav: note accent.

Mary Celeste

Mass (cap "M") but high Mass, etc, etc.

Massachusetts, thus.

massacre requires many dead, not merely a handful.

masterful (overwhelming), masterly (skilled).

matinee: no accent. See premiere.

MaxMara

May balls happen in June, at Cambridge.

mayor: John Smith, Mayor of Someville but later the mayor (lower case). Mayor of London, however, is capped.

Mbeki, Thabo

Macaulay, Sarah: Mrs Gordon Brown.

Macavity

Macbeth

MacKenzie, Kelvin

Mackintosh, Sir Cameron

MacLaine, Shirley

Maclean, Donald

Maclean, Alistair

Macleod, Iain

Macmillan, Harold

Macpherson, Elle

Macpherson Report on Stephen Lawrence.

McCain, John

McCartney, Sir Paul.

McDonald's

McDonald, Sir Trevor

McGregor, Ewan

McGuinness, Martin

McKellen, Sir Ian

McLaren, racing team.

McQueen, Alexander

Meat Loaf

Mecca: given this is Mohammed's birthplace, to describe somewhere like a nightclub as "a mecca for young people" risks causing grave offence to our Muslim readers.

medals: the Victoria Cross is the highest military honour for bravery. The civilian equivalent is the George Cross, which is followed by the George Medal.

Médecins Sans Frontières

media is a plural word which should be used only when newspapers, radio, television, press, broadcasting organisations and other precise terms are inaccurate or consume too much space in, say, an intro.

Medvedev, Dmitry

meet with is an abomination. See pointless prepositions.

Merchant Navy is capped in titles only, otherwise lower case.

merge with something, not into it.

Merkel, Angela

Messerschmitt. this is the way to spell the German manufacturer of Second World War fighter aircraft.

Messiah: Handel's oratorio does not take the handle "the".

meteoric rise: as well as being over-used, this is a bit silly when you consider what meteors do, i.e. hurtle towards Earth.

metrication: not metrification.

Michaeljohn: smart hairdresser.

Michelangelo

Mickey Mouse

micro light: not microlite.

Middle Ages – uc M, uc A, when describing the medieval period of history.

Middle East: Mideast only in headlines (see Places and Peoples). Middle West or Midwest.

Middle England: upper case when describing the conservative middle classes.

Midsummer's Day; a midsummer day.

mileage

militate is not to be confused with mitigate: the former means actively to counter something, the latter to moderate or make something less severe.

Millennium

million: in the business pages abbreviate to m, elsewhere in the paper always write out in full.

Milosevic, Slobodan

Minogue, Kylie's sister and erstwhile *X Factor* judge Dannii is spelt with a double n and double i.

minuscule is to be spelt correctly on the rare occasions when we need to refer to an early cursive script or small type, and on the rarer occasions when it can properly be used instead of small, tiny or minute.

miracles: biblical use only.

miss: the plural of this honorific is misses. So it is the Misses Smith, not the Miss Smiths.

Missouri, a Midwestern state in the US.

Mitterrand, François

mixed metaphors: be alert for these, such as "fuelling a backlash".

Mobutu, Sésé Séko

moderator (of a church) takes a capital in titles but later is lower case.

Moët et Chandon

mogul for Indian and other (e.g. film) references.

Mohammed is the Prophet, and use in all other contexts unless a variant is established in a personal name.

money: see Numbers file. For decimal denominations, place the point at the bottom, i.e. £14.95.

Mongol, in references to children suffering from Down's syndrome, offends.

Monroe, Marilyn

Moorfields

more, of two things (see comparatives).

mores, noun plural, the essential or characteristic customs and conventions of a society or community.

more than: much preferred to "over", so avoid "over 60 people".

morphed: never except in a strictly technical sense as a computer-generated special effect. Use "metamorphosed" in all other contexts.

Morrissey, Neil, is the actor. The former lead singer of The Smiths is known by his surname alone (though his Christian name is Steven).

mortgagee is the institution from which a mortgage is obtained: the person who takes it out is the mortgagor.

Mosimann, Anton

most requires at least three things (see superlatives).

mother of parliaments: never use to describe the parliament at Westminster. The phrase from which this much-misquoted line is taken is "England is the mother of parliaments".

motorcycle, motorcyclist

Mourinho, Jose, the self-styled special football coach.

mown is the perfect tense of mow. Not mowed.

MRSA: if this has to be written out in full it is methicillin-resistant Staphylococcus aureus.

MS and MSS for manuscript and manuscripts.

Mubarak, Hosni: former president of Egypt.

Muhammad Ali

mujahideen

multiculturalism

multiples: say "three times as many", not "three times more than". Never say "three times less than": you mean "one third of".

mum and dad are banned: mother and father is the right tone.

Mumbai (see Bombay).

Murdoch, Elisabeth

Musharraf, Pervez.

Muslim, not Moslem.

mutual, meaning common to two or more parties *(Our Mutual Friend)* should not be used unless the word common would be misleading or ambiguous.

Myriad, originally the Greek word for 10,000, requires no of: i.e. there are myriad people.

N

Nafta: North American Free Trade Agreement.

national anthems: lower case for the expression but caps for the titles of principal words in the title (the British national anthem is *God Save the Queen*).

national curriculum: lc.

National Farmers' Union

National Lottery is now also known as Lotto.

National Trust: a gift to the NT is not strictly a gift to the nation, so should not be described as such. Note: the trust is acceptable after first mention.

nationalists: cap only in references to parties which use the word in their titles and to their members. The Scottish National party has nationalist views and Scottish Nationalist candidates. Lower-case loyalists and republicans.

natives (for inhabitants) can offend.

nativity for the birth of Jesus.

Nato

NatWest: main bank or subsidiary (National Westminster Bank at first mention).

nearby in all uses.

negro, negress: do not use except in a clearly explained historical context.

Neil, Andrew

neither, see either.

neo-con is becoming rather tired. Use it only if you are going to show what it means.

neonatal (no hyphen)

Neptune/Pluto: Neptune was temporarily the Sun's most distant planet. Pluto's eccentric orbit brings it closer than Neptune every 248 years. This last happened between January 1979 and February 1999, whence it returned to its usual place as the ninth and most distant planet from the Sun.

nerve-racking

Network Rail: owns and operates all Britain's rail infrastructure.

nevertheless

new: appears more frequently than it should. It is needed sometimes but most readers would like to think that the plans, policies, inquiries we are telling them about are by definition new.

Newcastle upon Tyne

Newcastle-under-Lyme

New College, Oxford: do not omit college.

"new romantic"

newspaper: always thus, never just "paper".

newspaper proprietors: all references MUST be cleared with the editor or acting editor before appearing in the newspaper.

Newspaper Publishers Association: no apostrophe.

newspaper quotations: when reporting what foreign publications say, always indicate their political affiliations and how much authority they carry.

newspaper titles: are italicised and take the article if it is in their own masthead: i.e. *The Guardian, The Times, The Daily Telegraph,* etc but... *Daily Mail, Evening Standard.* Cap the "L" in the definite article in French titles (*Le Monde*); do not use "the" before the titles of foreign newspapers that include an article in their name (*Die Welt*). The suffixes -et or -en in Scandinavian titles are equivalent to "the".

New Year: caps for the festival (New Year's Day, New Year's Eve) but lower case for new year meaning the period about to begin. New Year's honours.

Nice, the National Institute for Health and Clinical Excellence, is the Government's medicines rationing watchdog.

Nicholson, Jack, but Nicolson, Harold, Nigel, Adam and Rebecca.

Nineteen Eighty-Four: the novel.

nitrobenzene: not-ine.

No: No 10 Downing Street, No 10: avoid elsewhere.

nom de plume is bad French. They would say *nom de guerre*.

none must be followed by a singular verb and singular pronoun: none of them was admitted to the room. None of them concede that they made mistakes is wrong, but such forms are used to avoid the clumsy "he or she". It can also be avoided by writing "none of them concedes that mistakes were made".

none the less

no one

northern hemisphere, the half of Earth that is north of the equator is written in lower case.

notwithstanding

now: use only to draw the distinction between past/future and present, otherwise the word is redundant.

number is always plural, despite being a singular noun: one would not say "a number of us is going to the pub". The same logic applies to other nouns describing a plurality, such as majority and minority: "a minority of doctors are alcoholics".

numbers: except in the City pages, the numbers one to nine are spelt out, after that they are given as numerals.

numskull: no b.

GLOSSARY

O

Obama, Barack

OBE does not stand for Order of the British Empire. It is Officer of the Most Honourable Order of the British Empire.

obligated is an Americanism and an abomination. There is nothing wrong with "obliged".

obscenity: always seek guidance in reporting foul language. It may be necessary to use a dash (not asterisks) to indicate the deletion of obscenity from direct quotes. Gratuitous use of obscenities is forbidden. The presumption must always be that profanities are forbidden.

occupied territories: lc.

Odinga, Raila: Kenyan politician.

of course: usually redundant and has the undesirable secondary effect of telling readers that a fact is known to everybody except ignoramuses such as them.

off: as a suffix to a verb it is often redundant, as in "sent off" when describing the posting of a letter. Think carefully before using.

offer: beware of the word offer in promotions. The company may be liable to compensation to anyone who ends up having a disastrous holiday that we have flagged as an offer.

offshore: no hyphen, nor in onshore.

offstage is a theatrical term and relates to something not visible to the audience of a production.

OK: only in quotes. Not Okay.

OK! the gossip magazine.

Old Etonian (cap O, E).

O-level: lc.

Olmert, Ehud: Israeli politician.

Olympic Games: the Games is an acceptable abbreviation.

on/in: on an island only when it is normally uninhabited or is too small to support more than a hamlet. On a desert island. In the Isle of Wight. In a ship, train, plane, bus. A shop in Oxford Street.

Ondaatje, Christopher or Michael.

one in four men takes a singular verb.

only should be placed next to the word it qualifies (he painted only the wall. Only he painted the wall).

opinion polls: always say who commissioned and conducted them, and who commissioned and conducted any survey or poll that might be mentioned in a story or feature. In polls commissioned by *The Daily Telegraph* always give the technical information about the sample and the dates of the interviews.

opposite to

Opposition is capped when referring to Her Majesty's Loyal Opposition, the second largest party in the House of Commons.

oral not verbal to make it plain that words were spoken.

orang-utan: note the hyphen.

ordeal is overworked.

Orders in Council: refers to orders by the Privy Council and should be capitalised.

ordinand is a candidate for the priesthood. An ordinee is one who has been ordained.

ordinary people: as the former cabinet minister Lord Falconer discovered to his cost, this term is interpreted as patronising or insulting. Avoid.

organic growth: in a business context this means "no-cost growth" or "low-cost growth", so is imprecise. Avoid outside quotes where possible.

orphan is a term that can correctly be applied to a person who has lost only one parent. Technically, one who has lost both is a double orphan.

Osama bin Laden, bin Laden at subsequent mentions.

Osbourne, Ozzy

Oscar: the award is capped.

other's: each other's.

outside of is an abomination. Children are born "outside marriage", not outside of it.

Outward Bound: is the registered trade mark of the Outward Bound Trust. Unless referring specifically to trust activities, use a term such as "outdoor pursuits". (See trade names.)

over may be used to mean "more than" if the structure of a sentence demands it, but should be avoided if possible.

overall is one word as an adjective.

overstatement is a curse. People are rarely devastated, horrified, stunned, outraged or amazed. Think carefully before attributing such characteristics to those about whom you are writing.

overwhelm should be treated with care as it means submerge utterly, crush, bring to sudden ruin.

P

Page 3 girls

Paglia, Camille

palate/palette/pallet. The first is the roof of the mouth in vertebrates. The second is a board on which an artist mixes colours. The third is a portable, mainly wooden platform on which goods are stacked and moved. It is also a makeshift bed.

Palestine Liberation Organisation (not Palestinian). PLO in heads and subsequent mentions. Explain which faction if possible.

Palmer-Tomkinson, Tara

pan is usually hyphenated e.g. pan-African. (But Pan Africanist Conference.)

panama: is a hat made not in Panama but Ecuador. As with trilby, boater, etc, "panama hat" is tautological

Panama cigar has a cap P.

paparazzi is the plural: paparazzo is the singular.

parallel

paranoia, this is a specific medical condition and not to be used to describe a person's sense of insecurity.

Parker Bowles, Brigadier Andrew: no hyphen.

partially, only in part, or favouring one side over another.

participles: "As result of him having eaten the cake, he had a heart attack" is wrong. If you use this construction, it has to include the possessive: "As a result of his having eaten the cake . . ."

partly, this adverb means to some extent; not completely nor partially, which means being inclined to favour one person or party: though partially sighted.

Parliament but parliamentary. Lower case when describing a particular term. Foreign parliaments are lc. See politics.

partner: To be used in the sense of a person's cohabitee when every other option is inappropriate . . . Use boy/girlfriend, lover, mistress, etc. Now that we have civil partnerships the term "civil partner" may be used about those who have undergone this legal ceremony with a member of the same sex. "Partner" may be used for a professional or business relationship.

Party (I): in the names of specific political parties it takes the cap P. The Labour Party, the Conservative Party but "all the parties were agreed".

party (II): its use as a verb (they partied until dawn) is ugly.

Pashtu is one of the languages of Afghanistan. Preferred to Pashto.

Pc: cap P, lc c. Strictly speaking, there are no WPcs now. They are women Pcs but WPc may be used in heads.

PCBs: polychlorinated biphenyls.

peal/peel, the former, a noun, is the sound of bells, thunder or both. The second, a verb, is to remove the skin or outer covering of a fruit, vegetable or whatever it is one is peeling.

Pearl Harbor: thus.

peddler/pedlar: use drug peddler (or trafficker), reserving pedlar for the more traditional meaning, a person who travels from place to place selling goods.

people not persons.

Pepsi-Cola

per cent does not take a point. Prefer seven in 10 people to 70 per cent of people.

percentage point is an Americanism though accepted use on the business pages. If interest rates rise from four to five per cent most people will see that as a rise of one per cent: technically, it is a rise of 25 per cent, hence the technical use of "one percentage point". To avoid either irritation or confusion, simply state the rise as "from four to five per cent", or describe the rise or fall in terms of basis points: a rise in rates from four to four and three-quarter per cent is a rise of 75 basis points".

Perestroika

perfume: use scent.

perk is acceptable for perquisite.

Pernod

personnel: avoid, and use people or employees.

Perspex: trade name, needs cap P; never use generically. (See trade names.)

persuade. to induce someone to do something through reasoned argument. (See convince.)

Peterhouse, Cambridge is never Peterhouse College.

Pfeiffer, Michelle

Philips: the electrical firm takes one l.

Piggott, Lester

Pimm's

PIN: Personal Identification Number. Not PIN number, i.e. Personal Identification Number number.

Pinocchio

Piper-Heidsieck

pistol is preferred to handgun. Say, if possible, if it is a revolver or an automatic. The two are frequently confused, and are not interchangeable. (See shotgun.)

pit bull terrier. No hyphen.

Play-Doh

PlayStation

plc is not to be routinely used after company names, though is of course permissible in technical contexts in describing the structure of companies.

plurals: follow the *Concise Oxford Dictionary* unless there is a contrary ruling in this style book.

Keep up with the Joneses, Rogerses, Charleses by refusing to use the Jones'. Proper names ending in -y do not end -ies in the plural (the Marys, Trilbys, laybys, zlotys). The Germanies are an exception.

Words ending in -a take the usual -s in the plural, except: alga, alumna, formula, lamina, larva, papilla, which take an -ae plural.

-ex and -ix endings become -ices only in appendices, calices, cortices, helices, radices. Indices only in mathematics and science. Indexes. Hexes. -is in words from Greek and Latin becomes -es: analyses, axes, oases.

Words ending in -o take -s (not -es) except: goes, heroes, noes, potatoes, salvoes (but salvos for excuses or reservations), tomatoes, tornadoes (but Tornados for the aircraft), torpedoes, vetoes, volcanoes.

Virtuosos, solos, sopranos, but normally -o words of Italian origins used mainly in the arts take -i in the plural.

-um in words from Latin becomes -a except for: referendums, compendiums, craniums, emporiums, mediums (but media as in mass media) memorandums, rostrums, stadiums.

-us in words from Latin becomes -i only in: alumni, bacilli, bronchi, cacti, calculi, foci (only in certain rare scientific terms), fungi, gladioli, loci, narcissi, nuclei, radii, stimuli, termini. Opus becomes opera. The normal form is geniuses, etc.

-criteria and phenomena are the plurals of criterion and phenomenon. You cannot have "a criteria".

Do not use an apostrophe to form the plural of a set of initials (MPs not MP's).

Poets' Corner.

pointless prepositions and other appendages: meet with is perhaps the most egregious example, but there is also sell off, tie up, free up, fence off, close down, fuse together, infringe upon, duck down, send off (a letter), rifle through, shut up (a building), print off and so on ad nauseam.

Always ask whether your preposition is really necessary. Nor does this always require a verb: "up until" is an abomination, as are "outside of" and "inside of".

police ranks: Commander, Chief Supt, Supt, Chief Insp, Insp, Sgt (Police Sgt if necessary to avoid confusion), Pc. Mr, Mrs or Miss may be used in second references to people above the rank of inspector. Dc, Det Sgt, Det Insp, Det Chief Insp, etc. See also Names and Titles.

policymaker, one word.

policy wonk: avoid. It is part of the private language of political obsessives, used to describe those who undertake political research, and like all private language alienates the general reader. See also ginger group and dog-whistle politics.

pollen, but pollinate.

poll tax

Pol Roger is the standard champagne, Pol Roger Cuvée Sir Winston Churchill the luxury brand.

Pontiff, the. Also the Pope.

Pontin's; note the apostrophe.

Porritt, Sir Jonathon

port, the fortified wine passes to the left.

Portakabin: is a trade name. Use "portable building" if you're not sure. (See trade names.)

possessives: nouns ending in -s add 's in the normal way (lass's, Charles's, St James's Square). To form the plural possessive, add an apostrophe to the -s of the plural (the lasses', The Joneses' dog). Names ending in -es pronounced -iz are treated as plurals (Bridges', Moses'). Jesus' is often found in biblical and liturgical use and should not be altered in quotations, but Jesus's is now normally preferred. Note the exception in for goodness' sake. Expressions like 10 years' jail and a pound's worth have apostrophes.

Apostrophes are needed in expressions in which words like shop or house are understood (going to the grocer's, going to Mr Brown's, but taking to the cleaners). This rule holds good for proper names (shopping at Marks and Spencer's), but when a business uses a title in plural form (Debenhams, Barclays Bank) no apostrophe is needed.

post, pre (meaning after and before) are prefixes, not whole words.

post mortem: means after death. We must say post mortem examination when we mean the means of determining cause of death.

postnatal

Post Office when referring to the company but post office for the place you go to buy stamps.

post-traumatic stress disorder

practice is a noun, practise is the verb.

pre-booked, pre-planned: avoid. See tautology.

pre-Budget report, thus.

pregnant: women become pregnant, never fall.

premiere: the first performance of a work does not require an accent.

Premiership is capitalised in the context of football. But the Blair premiership, for example.

prepositions at the ends of sentences are inelegant and should be avoided. Do not, though, avoid them at the cost of sounding ridiculous: remember Churchill's dictum about "this is the sort of English up with which I will not put".

presently is not now, it is soon. Use currently.

President Clinton/Bush: former US presidents keep their title. For all presidents, use full title the first time, then "Mr Sarkozy" thereafter. Lc when used in a generic context, but cap when used in a specific title with the person's name. E.g. President Barack Obama. But, the president of the United States.

press (for newspapers, reporters) is lower case.

prestigious in old usage it means deceitful, using sleight of hand. In modern usage it is mostly used to describe something admired or as having high status.

presume: see assume.

prevaricate does not mean to haver or procrastinate; it means to depart from the straight and narrow or to act crookedly or deceitfully.

preventive only in health stories: otherwise preventative.

priests are not necessarily Roman Catholics.

Prime Minister's Questions

Prince of Wales: not Prince Charles.

Princes Street, Edinburgh: no apostrophe.

Princess Royal, the: not Princess Anne.

principal/principle: the first is the main thing, or first in order of ranking, when an adjective. It is most commonly the most senior person in an organisation when a noun.

The second, a noun, is a fundamental truth or a proposition that serves as a foundation for a system of belief or behaviour.

prior to: avoid. Use before.

Privy Counsellor: not councillor.

prodigal. Spending money recklessly. A prodigal son or daughter is one who leads such a life but, normally, returns home repentant. (See also spendthrift.)

profanity: avoid. If in quotes you need to indicate that someone has used offensive language, enter a short dash for each letter of the word. An initial letter can be used only if there is room for misunderstanding.

profession is a term that can only correctly be applied to certain learned or chartered callings: the law, medicine, the civil service, teaching, accountancy for example. Other callings, such as journalism, are trades.

Professor: abbreviate to Prof before name, even at first use, but spell out in descriptions. Cap up when referring to a specific chair: Prof John Smith, Crippen Professor of Forensic Science, the Regius Professor of Law, Lord Smith, professor of history.

programme, but computer program.

propellant/ent: (n/adj) a propellant has a propellent effect.

propeller

protagonist: the chief actor in a drama, and by extension the main person in any affair. It does not mean champion, advocate or defender, and it is not the opposite of antagonist. There can only ever be one protagonist. Proponent may be a useful substitute.

protest requires the preposition "against": only American usage dispenses with this.

proved is to be preferred to the Americanism proven.

pub: this is perfectly acceptable for public house.

Public Record Office

Pullman carriage.

purl, to embroider.

Pyongyang: the capital of North Korea.

Q

QE2 for the liner.

quangos: Their names take capitals, immediately followed by bracketed acronym, and an acronym thereafter.

Queen: try to use "the Queen" in headlines.

Queen Elizabeth the Queen Mother is no longer. The title Queen Mother is one borne only for the lifetime of the holder, and may expire before that if her son or daughter the monarch predeceases her. We no longer refer to Queen Alexandra the Queen Mother (as she was from 1910 to 1925) or Queen Mary the Queen Mother (as she was from 1936 to George VI's death in 1952), and by the same token the last occupant of the post is now Queen Elizabeth. In copy, it is permissible to refer to her at first mention as "the late Queen Elizabeth the Queen Mother", in case of any confusion with the present sovereign: who is always the Queen. Thereafter, having established whom we are talking about, Her late Majesty is always to be "Queen Elizabeth".

Queen's Christmas message, every December 25. The Queen's Speech is at the State Opening of Parliament.

Queens' College Cambridge, The Queen's College Oxford, Queen's University Belfast.

question: no question but that = no doubt that. No question of = no possibility of. It is correct but ambiguous to write "no question that" or "no question but". Best avoid.

question marks: do not forget them. Make sure, too, that the verb before the question is not "said". A sentence ending with a question mark does not further require a full point.

quite means something quite different in America. Here it means comparatively or rather; there it means very.

quotation marks: use double quotes except in heads, captions or crossheads. Quotes within quotes are single; quotes within quotes within quotes are double. Quotes starting with a colon end with a full stop inside the close quote as in — Mr Smith said: "Yes, I did it." Quotes without a colon start end with the close quote inside the full point, as in — abusive telephone calls warned him he would "not live long".

R

racket and racquet: a tennis player uses his racquet while the fans make a racket.

radiologist/radiographer, the former is medically qualified and deals with X-rays and high-energy radiation in the treatment of diseases. The latter helps take the images for an examination and diagnosis and is not so well qualified.

rainforest

Raleigh, Sir Walter

Ramblers' Association

Ray-Ban

R&D, not R and D.

raze to the ground: to destroy completely (a building or structure).

real estate: use property instead.

reason: the noun should be followed by that, not why.

rebut: to offer evidence supporting a contrary view.

reconnaissance, noun, military observation. Double n; double s.

records, unless qualified, are presumed to be "all-time". Do not say that somebody set a new record. New is understood.

recycling, noun. The conversion of waste into reusable material.

redaction is editing, not censorship.

Rees-Mogg

referendums: not referenda. And later, a "yes" vote or a "no" vote. Also stadiums, not stadia. (See plurals.)

refute does not mean deny or reply to. It means disprove, and, therefore, means the writer has decided who is telling the truth. Rebut, for similar reasons, is best left to the lawyers.

Regent's Park

register office, not registry.

relations, not relatives.

relationship: a vague and overused word now. If you have to use it, say "the relationship of John and Mary" rather than "the relationship between John and Mary".

Remembrance Sunday. There is no such day as Remembrance Day.

repertory, a repository. A repertory theatre has a repository or repertoire of plays and a stock of actors.

reported speech: news stories should be written in reported speech, including write-offs of interviews, but not interviews themselves.

Republic, Irish, but Irish republican.

restaurateur

Resurrection requires a capital R in a biblical context.

retail prices index (RPI).

retired: Lt-Col John Smith retd. Field Marshals, Admirals of the Fleet and Marshals of the RAF never retire, and no officer below the rank of Major in the Army would ever use his rank in civilian life. Do not use the service rank of anyone below the rank of squadron leader in the RAF or lieutenant commander in the Royal Navy for a retired officer.

Reuters

reveal is tabloid: use disclose, sparingly.

Reverend in a person's title is always abbreviated Rev, not Revd: and it requires either a Christian name or an honorific after it: i.e., the Rev John Smith, the Rev Mr Smith, the Rev Dr Smith, but never the Rev Smith.

Rhys Jones, Griff. Any reference to the family of the Countess of Wessex is to Rhys-Jones.

Rice, Condoleezza

Richter scale: scale of measurement often used to assess extent of earthquakes. Also Mercalli scale, used to measure earthquake intensity from one to 12 (catastrophic). Superseded by the Moment scale of magnitude (MMS). Be clear which is being used.

Richtofen, Baron Manfred von

Right/Left: capped as political terms. Right-winger. But use with care.

Riley, life of.

"Rime of the Ancient Mariner"

rivers: usually take just their name and do not need "river". The Windrush, the Blackwater.

Rogers, Lord: architect.

Rodgers and Hammerstein

Rolls-Royce: with hyphen, whether cars or aircraft engines.

role has no circumflex accent.

Roller-blade is a trade name.

Roman Catholic always at first mention.

romance is not a verb.

Romania, not Rumania.

Roman numerals: these may be used to describe sporting teams. For example: the England XI, the Welsh XV, the Trinity VIII. They may also be used to differentiate generations of families where that is the family's preferred usage, for example John Smith I and John Smith II. Other than monarchs and other highly specialised usages they should be avoided.

rosé: takes an accent in reference to wine.

rottweilers

round and around: "round" is specific as in "he went round the world/block/park". "Around" is non-specific as in "he wandered around the world/block/park".

Rovers Return (no apostrophe).

Royal family, Royal household, but royal visit, royal children, royal corgis. The Royal Yacht Britannia, but the royal yacht. The royal standard is flown to denote the presence of the sovereign. Other members of the Royal family have banners. Royal household is the establishment that serves the Royal family, and is not synonymous with it. The terms "a Royal" and "the Royals" are to be avoided at all times. Prefer "a member of the Royal family" and "the Royal family".

Royal, Ségolène

Rubik's cube

rue de Remarques: all French street terms are lower case.

Rule, Britannia – note the comma.

S

Saakashvili, Mikheil, President of Georgia.

safe haven is a tautology.

said: is a neutral word, unlike some of the alternatives. To say that somebody claimed that something was true implies doubt; "pointed out that" implies agreement. Newspapers sometimes say that a man "admitted that", although he thought he had merely "agreed that" or "accepted that".

Do not use the construction "He said:" or "She said:" at the front of a paragraph. It implies we already know who is speaking and is thus redundant, as well as being an unnecessary intrusion on the reader's train of thought. If needed, the speaker's presence may be reinforced by adding "he/she said" at the end of the paragraph.

Sainsbury's

Saint: abbreviated to St (no point); plural is SS (SS Peter and Paul). (See Places and Peoples.)

Saint Laurent, Yves

Saint-Saëns, Camille (note umlaut).

St Andrews

St Bartholomew's Hospital may be shortened to Barts but never St Barts or St Bart's.

St George's Chapel, Windsor.

St James's Palace

St John Ambulance

St John's wort

St Thomas' Hospital

Salt (Strategic Arms Limitation Talks): Use Salt-1, Salt-2 for rounds of meetings and treaties.

Sam-5, Sam-6 for Soviet surface-to-air missiles.

Sana'a, capital of Yemen.

Santa: we use Father Christmas.

Sarkozy, Nicolas

Satan: cap S but satanic is lower case.

satnav

Saudi Arabia: note that Saudi on its own is an adjective and not an acceptable noun for the country.

Savile for Lord, Row, Club and Sir Jimmy. Saville Theatre and Inquiry. Savills estate agency.

Scalextric

Schiffer, Claudia

Schleswig-Holstein-Sonderburg-Glücksburg, thus.

Schönberg, Arnold – note the umlaut.

schoolboy, schoolgirl, but school-leaver.

Schumacher, Michael

Schwarzenegger, Arnold

Scorsese, Martin

scotch whisky, pies, pines, mists, eggs and wool shops. Scots or Scottish preferred in other contexts.

Scottish offshore islands: never "the Shetlands" or "the Orkneys". "The Shetland Islands" or "the Orkney Islands" is acceptable, but try to name the specific island, e.g "the Orkney island of Hoy".

Scots Porage Oats. Prisoners do porridge.

Scott Thomas, Kristin

Scouts, not Boy Scouts. Scout leaders not Scoutmasters. The Scout Association: note definite article.

sea change is not a complete change, but an unexpected one. It is overused as an expression.

Sea Lords: they used to work at the Admiralty.

seasonable: appropriate for the time of year, opportune.

seasonal: occurring regularly at a particular season (see spring).

Sebag Montefiore, Simon. His wife is Santa Montefiore.

Second World War not World War Two.

secretary-general of the UN.

see: only an animate object can see anything. Avoid tabloid usages such as "last year saw a sharp increase in the number of deaths" where saw is a lazy substitute for resulted in, caused or simply "there were".

Seinfeld, Jerry

Selfridges

senior and junior after American names should be snr and jnr.

sentence construction: make sure your nouns and pronouns match up. Thus "having been ill for weeks, Sir John received a visit from the Queen" is correct, but "having been ill for weeks, the Queen went to see John" is not — unless the Queen is the invalid.

Services. The Services takes the cap S, servicemen do not.

serviette: use napkin.

sewerage/sewage: sewerage is the pipes, sewage the stuff.

sex: avoid the expression "having sex". Use the full phrase "having sexual intercourse".

Shakespearean, not Shakespearian.

shalwar kameez: singular, like suit.

Shankill Road

sharia law is a tautology: Islamic law is not.

shear: something is shorn off, or shears off: it never sheers off.

sheikh, sheikhdom

Shepard, EH: illustrator of *Winnie the Pooh*.

Shepherd, Cybill

Shepherd's Bush

Shia is the noun and the adjective.

shih-tzu

shippers are people who consign cargo. They are not ship-owners.

ships: they are of female gender, i.e. she. People serve in a ship, not on it. Use HMS before names of naval vessels.

Short, Clare

shotgun: know the difference between a shotgun, a sporting weapon which fires lead shot, and a rifle, which fires bullets. Their capabilities and the damage they can inflict are very different. Firearm is the generic term.

show: be thoughtful in using this verb. Activities that we claim "show" something — that is, prove it beyond doubt — often do nothing of the kind. They might indicate, or suggest, but they are very different matters.

Shrops is the abbreviation for Shropshire, not Salop.

shut: avoid "shut down" as a verb. Shut-down (n) is useful for cessation of output.

sieve, a mesh utensil.

Sikora, Karol, cancer expert.

Sikorsky (helicopters), Sikorski (Polish leader).

silhouette, a dark outline.

silicon is the element from which chips are made: silicone is the Pamela Anderson substance.

simply: this has become a meaningless grunt in many sentences, for example "I simply don't know what to do". Avoid.

Simpson's-in-the-Strand

Sindy doll

ski, skier, skied, skiing.

slashed is tabloid: use cut or reduced.

smelt not smelled.

soar: do not use as a metaphor for rise. It is usually an exaggeration. (See crash.)

Socialist: cap only in descriptions of people directly associated with parties calling themselves Socialist, Lower case for socialist ideals, principles, etc. Not to be used of the Labour Party.

some in front of a numeral — "some 200 people" — adds nothing.

somebody, someone: single words.

sorted is what objects or abstracts are when they have been categorised into groups. The resolution of a problem is when something is sorted out.

Sotheby's: with apostrophe.

sound bite is two words.

southern hemisphere: the southern hemisphere is the part of Earth south of the equator. It takes lower case.

sparked is a lazy way of saying provoked.

Speaker of the House of Commons: always capped. Note that John Bercow is the current one.

spearheading means leading. Use sparingly and usually in a military context.

Special Boat Service

speciality: this applies to something that is particular to a certain person, business or institution. The specific discipline of a doctor is a specialty.

spendthrift, such a person is profligate, not parsimonious. (See also prodigal.)

Spielberg, Steven

spilt not spilled.

spin doctor: best used only ironically, ditto the verb to spin in this context.

spiralling: this term is now so overused that it is becoming meaningless, as in phrases such as "spiralling oil prices". Avoid.

split infinitives are not a mortal sin, but most can and should be avoided. Be guided by the relative ease of understanding. To boldly go easily becomes to go boldly, or even boldly to go. (See infinitives).

spoilt but despoiled.

stadiums, not stadia.

spokesman: not spokeswoman, spokesperson. Also, foreman as in foreman of the jury.

spring, summer, autumn, winter are lower-case.

staggering: use only literally, not metaphorically.

staging is to be preferred to hosting a big event: London stages the Olympics, but a person hosts a dinner party.

state: lower case except when part of a title (State President, Council of State, but state-owned).

stationary: not moving.

stationery: writing paper.

statistics, it is our style to say statistics suggest something rather than show it.

stem cell research has no hyphens.

stiletto, plural stilettos.

storm: use only in its literal sense.

Stratford upon Avon: see gazetteer. But Stratford-on-Avon district council and Stratford upon Avon town council. Check own websites.

strike, not strike action.

struck off: erring doctors or solicitors should be said to be "ordered to be struck off" until the time allowed for appeals has expired.

subjunctive: the verbal mood expressing something imagined, wished or possible.

summit: lower case. Do not use for any meeting by senior politicians, but reserve for talks at which leaders of important nations try to solve problems which their subordinates have failed to overcome. "Mini-summit" should be avoided.

sun: cap only in (rare) references to it as a star. The sun is out, our sun is one of many suns, the distance between the Sun and Alpha Major is . . .

***Sunday Times* Rich List**

Sunni

super: as in star, brat, mum, etc is repellently tabloid.

superlatives are used when comparing three or more things: the best player; the eldest child. (See comparatives)

swap: preferred to swop.

swashbuckler is not a daredevil but a swaggering bully.

swath: a strip.

swathe is a verb.

swearing: see obscenity.

sweet is a food that is not savoury. The course before cheese (or after it in France) is pudding.

T

T: have something down to a T.

T-shirts

tablespoonful(s)

tad is banned.

Taittinger

Taliban

take, as in "a new take on . . ." is hackneyed.

Taki Theodoracopulos

Taoiseach: the prime minister of the Irish Republic.

target is not a verb.

task is not a verb.

taste: good manners rather than political correctness dictate that we should be sensitive in using certain words to describe afflictions. Words such as cripple, spastic or dumb must never be used. It is one thing to describe a public figure who does something idiotic as a nutter, quite another to use that term to describe someone who is mentally ill. Exercise your discretion at all times.

tautology: like pointless prepositions (qv) there are many examples, such as "potential risk" (all risk is) and "could potentially" (the adverb is redundant) and "pre-planned" and "pre-booked" (which speak for themselves). Always ponder whether your adverb is really necessary. A frequent mistake is "relatively small compared with" in which relatively is unnecessary.

Tchaikovsky, Pyotr

tea-bags

teams: England have lost the Ashes is now the accepted idiomatic use; as it is that West Ham have been relegated. When talking about the single entity of a sports club, however, use the singular, as in "the club has today announced the appointment of its new chairman".

Teasmade

teenage, teenager, not teenaged and never teen.

Teesside

Tehran

telecoms is acceptable for headlines and in the business section; elsewhere it should be telecommunications.

Telegraph.co.uk

telephone: thus, as a noun or a verb, though mobile phone is acceptable.

telephone numbers: when giving a British telephone number follow this formula:
(020) 7931 2000 and (01234) 123456.

temperatures: give Fahrenheit figure followed by Celsius (now preferred to centigrade) in this style: 60F (16C). No point. No degree sign. Temperatures rise by 15 degrees; they do not get warmer by 15 degrees.

Tennents: lager.

tenses: avoid confusing these. Avoid captions such as "the Queen arrives at Heathrow yesterday".

Teresa, Mother

terrace: terrace house, not terraced.

Terrence Higgins Trust

terrestrial: not terrestial (no such word).

terror is not a synonym for terrorism. The latter arouses the former.

Terry-Thomas had a hyphen.

that: after verbs like "said" and "thought" the conjunction can be omitted unless "and that" is required in the second half of a sentence, in which case two "thats" are needed (the reporter said that the sub-editor was mad and that, if he cut his copy again, he would beat him).

that/which: use which in clauses that add incidental, but not essential information; prefer that in restrictive or defining clauses. Note the difference between "the dog that I saw was black" and "the dog, which I saw, was black". The first refers specifically to a dog that I saw — distinct from a dog anyone else saw — being black. The second emphasises the fact that I saw a dog.

the then: this usage as in "Lady Thatcher, the then prime minister" is to be avoided. Prefer "the prime minister at the time".

The Times — two cap T's.

think tank: often misused for research group, advisers or pressure group. Not purged by the use of quotation marks.

Third Reich, the.

Third World

Thompson, Emma

Three-line whip

Tiananmen Square

Tiffany's

till is to be avoided except in quotations. Prefer until.

toddler: aptly describes children from the age of about 15 months to three.

toe the line, not tow.

toilet: use only to describe the personal cleansing regime. The object is a lavatory.

Toksvig, Sandi

Tolkien, J R R

ton is imperial; tonne is metric. Use the former, given our preference for imperial measurements, except in specific scientific stories. The two sizes are sufficiently close to avoid confusion.

top: avoid using as an adjective in phrases such as "top judges" or **"top jockeys"**.

Topshop

total is not a verb.

Trade Descriptions Act

trade names require caps and should be avoided as much as possible. Watch particularly for words that are not obviously trade names. This list contains only a few of the hundreds of trade names in regular use: Autogiro, Biro (ballpoint pen), Cashpoint, Caterpillar tractor (tracked tractor), Catseye (reflecting stud), Cellophane (transparent wrapping), Dictaphone (dictating machine), Formica (plastic top), Granary (bread), Hoover (vacuum cleaner), iPod, iPhone, iPad, Jeep (crosscountry vehicle, but jeep is used in references to the wartime vehicle). Perspex (acrylic sheet), Photostat (photo-copy), Plasticine (modelling material), Sellotape, Tabloid (for tablets; tabloid for a newspaper is acceptable), Tannoy (loudspeaker), Thermos (vacuum flask), Valium, Vaseline (petroleum jelly), Yale lock (cylinder-rim locks for other makes). Many words starting with tele- (but not telex) are trade names in communications. The Oxford dictionaries identify many words with the warning "P". There is also a government search engine for UK registered trade marks at www.ipo.gov.uk/tm.

trade union, trade unions but Trades Union Congress.

tragedy: grotesquely and inappropriately overused. If it is deployed to describe the unfortunate death of a person in a car crash, what word is to be used to describe a holocaust?

train: comprises the locomotive and carriages or wagons.

tranquillity: (double L) is our style.

treasure trove: a coroner's court may declare that a find is treasure trove if it is held that the gold or silver was originally hidden with a view to being recovered later. In this case the finder may be compensated. If the treasure is deemed to have been lost accidentally, the finder can keep it.

Tricolor is the French flag.

Trooping the Colour (no of). It means parading the colour before the troops. Also Beating Retreat (no the).

"trouble in paradise": a cliché that should never be used in stories or headlines about exotic places, Caribbean islands, etc.

Troubles the, referring to Northern Ireland.

try and is wrong: it is try to.

tsar: not czar.

Tussaud's, Madame

Tutu, Archbishop Desmond

TV: only in headlines.

Twentieth Century Fox

twin-set

twitchers/bird-watchers: "twitchers" are enthusiasts whose main interest is seeing as many rare species as possible. More traditional bird-watchers tend to be sedate and observe the birds and their habits.

Tymoshenko, Yulia — the former Prime Minister of Ukraine.

U

uber as the prefix to an English noun was funny a decade ago, but is past its sell-by date now.

UK: do not use to mean Great Britain. (See Places and Peoples.)

Ulysses

umlauts: German words should retain umlauts at all times and not have an 'e' inserted to lengthen the vowel.

UN: spell out United Nations at first mention in text. UN Security Council takes caps.

under way, not underway or under weigh.

Underground is capped when describing the London transport system.

underwhelmed used to be funny, but no longer.

unforeseeable

unfrocked/defrocked: our style is unfrocked.

UNHCR: the United Nations High Commissioner for Refugees.

Union: when describing Great Britain and Northern Ireland, it should be capped.

Union Jack: properly, this is for the flag's naval use only (when flown from a jackstaff) and in all other contexts it should be the Union flag.

unique: if you do use it remember that it cannot be qualified.

United Kingdom: this refers to the nation formed by England, Scotland, Wales and Northern Ireland. England, Scotland and Wales form Great Britain. Great Britain and the island of Ireland form the British Isles.

United Reformed Church: not Reform.

United States, then US.

university departments do not take caps unless they contain proper nouns.

Unknown Warrior: it is he, and not the Unknown Soldier, who lies in Westminster Abbey.

unprecedented: see unique.

unself-conscious

upcoming: Americanism. Use "forthcoming".

V

Valium

Vaughan Williams, Ralph: no hyphen, never Williams.

venerable is not a synonym for old. It means worthy of reverence.

verbal, unlike oral, refers to written as well as spoken words. Verbal agreement is a tautology as all agreements are verbal. If you mean one that is not subsequently recorded in writing, say oral agreement.

verbs: should always agree in number with the proceeding subject or subjects. In long sentences — which themselves should be avoided — pay extra attention to ensure that nouns and verbs agree.

verruca, an unpleasant foot wart. It is spelt with two rs and one c.

very: usually redundant.

vet: acceptable for veterinary surgeon (but note spelling of the full-out word for describing colleges, professional bodies).

Veuve Clicquot: note the c in the middle.

vibrant: tired, and never to be used in the hackneyed sense of describing an ethnic mix.

vicar is a specific post in the Church of England. It is not to be used generically for "clergyman". Some C of E parish clergy are rectors. In the past they received twice the amount of the tithe as vicars.

vice-president

Vicks: no apostrophe.

victims: use sparingly.

Victorian: Queen Victoria reigned from 1837-1901.

Virgin Birth

Vodafone

Volkswagen

Vorderman, Carol

vow, only to be used in a religious context.

W

Wales: South Wales, North Wales, West Wales, Mid Wales.

Walesa, Lech

Wallace and Gromit

Wal-Mart

Wanamaker, Zoë

-ward, wards. "Yet man is born unto trouble, as the sparks fly upward" is how the King James Bible has it. Contemporary usage, however, suggests that when it is an adjective a word like upward, downward, backward or forward should not end in s, but when it is an adverb it should. For example: "homeward bound", "the upward and the downward slope", "forward planning", but "spread outwards", "peer downwards", "move forwards".

warn: "He warned that . . ." is wrong. The speaker must warn somebody or "give a warning that."

wars: caps when there is a recognised title; the Vietnam War, First World War (or 1914-18 War), the Second World War (or 1939-45) War. But not World War 2 or other variations. The term the Great War to describe the First World War is not incorrect, but should be confined to feature writing. Where war is not declared use lc w or find another term, e.g. Falklands war or Falklands conflict. We should also refer to the first Iraq war (1991) and the second Iraq war (2003).

Waterstone's

wealthy: use rich.

weather is enough: we do not need to say weather conditions.

website and webmaster. But web page and web server.

Weight Watchers

welfare state

Wellcome Trust, the world's leading medical research charity: not Welcome.

wellington boot: lower case. (see caesarean section).

West is capped for recognised regions and in political contexts but not as a point of the compass.

West Country

whether: see if.

whisky for Scotch whisky, whiskey for others. Do not refer to whisky as Scotch, always Scotch whisky.

which and that: which informs, that defines. This is the house that Jack built, but: this house, which Jack built, is now falling down.

Whitaker's Almanack

White Paper

Whiteread, Rachel

whizkid

who, whom: choice is dictated by the word's function within a clause. Do not be misled by the intrusion of phrases such as "he said" between the pronoun and the verb. "The reporter, who the editor said was mad, smiled" is correct. "Who" is the subject in the clause with the verb "was". "The reporter, whom the editor described as mad, smiled" is also correct. "Whom" is the object of the verb "described".

Widdecombe, Ann

widow: a woman whose husband has died, and has not remarried. It is incorrect to call such a woman a wife. A widow is also an unsightly short last line at the end of a paragraph falling at the top of a page or column of print.

Widow Twankey

Wi-Fi is a tradename, with caps.

wills: do not be misled by the gross total. The net figure is the one to use in heads like "MP leaves £250,000".

wines: when writing about wine regions, do not use caps. So, write white burgundy, red bordeaux, pink champagne, cognac. However, when writing about geographical regions or places, then use caps as for all other proper names. Therefore write a visit to Burgundy, a hotel in Bordeaux, the villages of Champagne and the mayor of Cognac. Grape varieties are all lower case. Rosé takes an accent.

Winslet, Kate

Wirral; no the.

Wisden Cricketers' Almanack

Woolf, Virginia and Leonard

Woolworths

world: avoid tired usages such as the fashion world, the theatre world.

World Heritage Site

World Trade Center

World Wide Fund for Nature

worth: millions of pounds' worth.

Wreaked/wrought: the past tense of wreak is wreaked. Iron may be wrought (old past tense of work) or prose finely wrought, but havoc is wreaked.

X

Xmas: never use. Ditto Yule.

Y

Yahoo! has an exclamation mark.

years: 2006–07, not 2006/7.

Yes, Minister

yesterday: use sparingly in news stories. It is rarely necessary, and confusing for internet readers.

Yeti, a mythological large, hairy bear-like creature.

yogurt: not yoghurt.

YouGov: thus.

youngster is tabloid.

youth only applicable to a young man.

YouTube, thus.

Yushchenko, Viktor: the former president of Ukraine.

Z

Zeffirelli

Zeta Jones, Catherine